Better Homes and Gardens®

EASY beading

jewelry • beadmaking • decorations

Meredith® Books
Des Moines, Iowa

Better Homes and Gardens®
EASY
beading
jewelry • beadmaking • decorations

Editor: Carol Field Dahlstrom
Writer: Susan M. Banker
Designer: Catherine Brett
Technical Assistant: Judy Bailey
Copy Chief: Terri Fredrickson
Copy and Production Editor: Victoria Forlini
Publishing Operations Manager: Karen Schirm
Managers, Book Production: Marjorie J. Schenkelberg, Rick von Holdt, Mark Weaver
Contributing Copy Editor: Arianna McKinney
Contributing Proofreaders: Julie Cahalan, Karen Brewer Grossman, Sara Henderson
Photographers: Andy Lyons Cameraworks, Scott Little, Jay Wilde
Photostyling Assistant: Donna Chesnut
Technical Illustrator: Shawn Drafahl
Editorial and Design Assistants: Kaye Chabot, Mary Lee Gavin, Karen McFadden

Meredith® Books

Publisher and Editor in Chief: Linda Raglan Cunningham
Design Director: Matt Strelecki
Executive Editor, Food and Crafts: Jennifer Dorland Darling

Publisher: James D. Blume
Executive Director, Marketing: Jeffrey Myers
Executive Director, New Business Development: Todd M. Davis
Executive Director, Sales: Ken Zagor
Director, Operations: George A. Susral
Director, Production: Douglas M. Johnston
Business Director: Jim Leonard

Vice President and General Manager: Douglas J. Guendel

Better Homes and Gardens® Magazine

Editor in Chief: Karol DeWulf Nickell

Meredith Publishing Group

President, Publishing Group: Stephen M. Lacy
Vice President-Publishing Director: Bob Mate

Meredith Corporation

Chairman and Chief Executive Officer: William T. Kerr

In Memoriam: E. T. Meredith III (1933–2003)

All of us at Meredith® Books are dedicated to providing you with information and ideas to create beautiful and useful projects. We welcome your comments and suggestions. Write to us at: Meredith Books, Crafts Editorial Department, 1716 Locust Street—LN112, Des Moines, IA 50309-3023.

If you would like to purchase any of our crafts, cooking, gardening, home improvement, or home decorating and design books, check wherever quality books are sold. Or visit us at: bhgbooks.com

contents

beautiful
beading

Welcome to a world of beading inspiration, where you'll discover beaded treasures to wear or adorn your home.

Beads make us feel beautiful, whether we wear them as jewelry or use them to embellish our homes. These small pieces of sparkling glass, colorful acrylic, smooth bone, textured clay, and shiny metal are like magic as they come together to form art pieces for us to enjoy. We string them on wire, plastic, linen, and countless other materials and we sew or glue them on just about everything. However we choose to enjoy them, they add beauty and loveliness to our lives.

In this book of easy beading ideas, we show you how to make beads, string beads, and decorate with beads. From elegant chokers and clever bracelets to beaded valances and simple bookmarks, we offer you a variety of ways to use the amazing selection of beads available.

Take advantage of these lovely and tiny works of art and use your creative talents to fashion some beautiful beading.

Carol Field Dahlstrom

Editor

beads for all time

Beading is back in style.

As crafters today, we are enjoying a resurgence in the interest of beading. What fun to have store after store offer bins of unusual and elegant beads just waiting for us to take home to create our own works of art. We can find all the colors and supplies we could ever dream of, and we can even make our own beads using the glass supply kits and materials so readily available.

Beading has been around for centuries. In every culture—from the Stone Age and Africa to Native American tribes and the Victorian era—beads have been used to add color, vitality, and personality to clothing and household items.

The earliest beads were made of seeds, pods, stones, wood, teeth, and bone fragments. Glass beads have been found in Egyptian royal graves of the 21st century BC.

The word *bead* comes from *bede*, a Middle English word meaning a "prayer." On an abacus, beads are moved to add and subtract. In some eras, beads have served as wampum (which means "a string of white beads"), or currency, or were used for symbolic purposes, depending on how the beads were arranged on a string. Sometimes beads were believed to help ward off evil spirits.

Holding the possibility of limitless designs, beads have come in a myriad of shapes, sizes, colors, and materials over the years, including gems, wood, pearl, metal, plastic, and glass. Historical glass bead making came primarily from Venice and Murano, Italy.

Often beaded items had special messages woven into the patterns, even beaded "love letters."

Certain colors signified meanings. White beads conveyed love, and yellow symbolized wealth. Red showed anger, and blue meant departure. In the time of Columbus, beads were traded for furs. Woodland and Plains Indians, who previously only used dyed porcupine quills for ornamentation, were able to add beads. Later tribes became known for their distinctive beaded designs—Lake Indians for flowered designs; Sioux or Plains for geometric; Blackfoot and northern plains for larger geometric patterns. For pure beauty, few could top the intricate detail of the Apaches.

In the late 1800s, with personal adornment a must, Victorians perfected the art of beading in ornate pins, brooches, purses, hair combs, and hat pins. Prized jet beads were woven into necklaces worn during times of mourning in the 1800s.

First Ladies often chose Inaugural Ball gowns embellished with intricate beadwork. Caroline Scott Harrison (1889–1892) wore a dress with collar and trim at the waist in gold and silver beading. President Harrison's daughter, Mary McKee, wore a satin brocade gown, embellished with silver and amber beads. Helen Herron Taft (1909–1913) sent her white silk chiffon dress to Tokyo, Japan, for embroidery in silver thread and crystal beads.

In many parts of Africa, men and women wear beads in fancy headpieces and lavish earrings. In some areas, girls wear beaded aprons in bright geometric designs. On their upper bodies, women might hang bunches of beads and intricately beaded neck collars.

Today beaded jewelry and other decorative beaded pieces provide interest and fun for all ages. Colorful bead shops provide choices from around the world as beads continue to charm and fascinate us with their sparkle and magic.

Bibliography on page 111

beading basics

Whether you're new to the art of beading or have a master's degree in crimping, this helpful section guides you through the basics so your beaded projects turn out with professional style.

millefiori-style beads

silver bugle beads

taper beads

beads of every kind

colored bugle beads

This sampling shows a few of the beautiful types of beads available for your projects. Hundreds of bead types range from tiny glass seed beads to large wire spirals.

shaped cane glass beads

bumpy glass beads

drum beads

chip beads

twisted tube beads

leaf and flower glass beads

disk glass beads

opaque glass beads

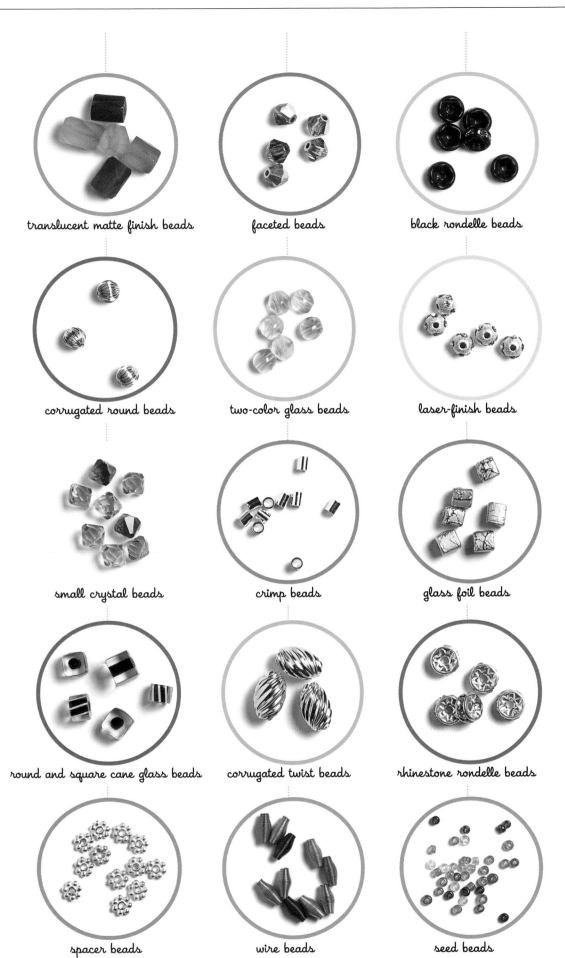

translucent matte finish beads

faceted beads

black rondelle beads

corrugated round beads

two-color glass beads

laser-finish beads

small crystal beads

crimp beads

glass foil beads

round and square cane glass beads

corrugated twist beads

rhinestone rondelle beads

spacer beads

wire beads

seed beads

other findings and tools you need

Round up beads and some basic supplies to prepare for just about any beading project.

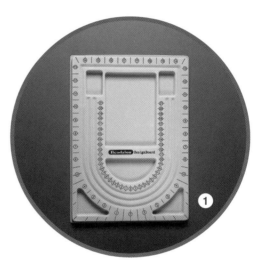

①

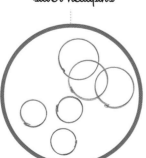

silver headpins

spring ring clasps

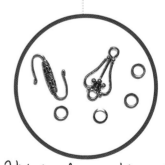

Victorian clasps and jump rings

wire hoops

toggle and lobster clasps

filigree clasps

1 **Beading tray**—The plastic tray has channels in it to assist with bead arrangement.

2 **Flush wire cutters**—Cut wires of various thicknesses by clamping down on wire to create a smooth end.

3 **Round-nose pliers**—These pliers grab wire, which is wrapped around the nose of the pliers to form spirals in the wire.

4 **Split ring pliers**—This handy tool opens split rings.

5 **Elastic cord**—Created for making jewelry, this elastic is available in different sizes and comes in clear and limited colors.

6 **Suede lacing**—Available in a variety of colors, this lacing is flat with the rough surface of suede.

7 **Round leather lacing**—Available in several colors, this lacing is thin with a smooth surface.

how to crimp

When connecting your beaded strings to clasps, crimp beads make the process easy and the connection secure.

what you'll need

Wire cutters
Beading wire
Crimp beads
Crimping tool
Desired clasp

here's how

1 Gather the supplies listed, *above*.

2 Cut the beading wire to the length instructed in the project directions.

3 Thread a crimp bead on one end of beading wire, pass wire through the end of the desired clasp, and run wire back through the crimp bead in the opposite direction as shown in Photo A, *opposite*. (Note: The crimping tool has two notches, one to flatten the crimp bead and one to round out the flattened crimp.) Flatten the crimp bead firmly with a crimping tool as shown in Photo B. Squeeze crimp bead again to round out the bead. Trim the end with wire cutters if needed. (For a closer view see Photo C.)

4 After the wire is beaded, repeat Step 3 to attach the remaining piece of clasp.

5 Cut the wire ends close to the crimp beads and tuck the ends into the adjacent beads.

crimp beads

crimping tool

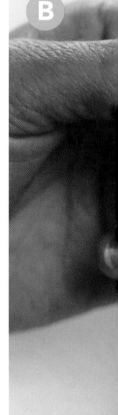

B

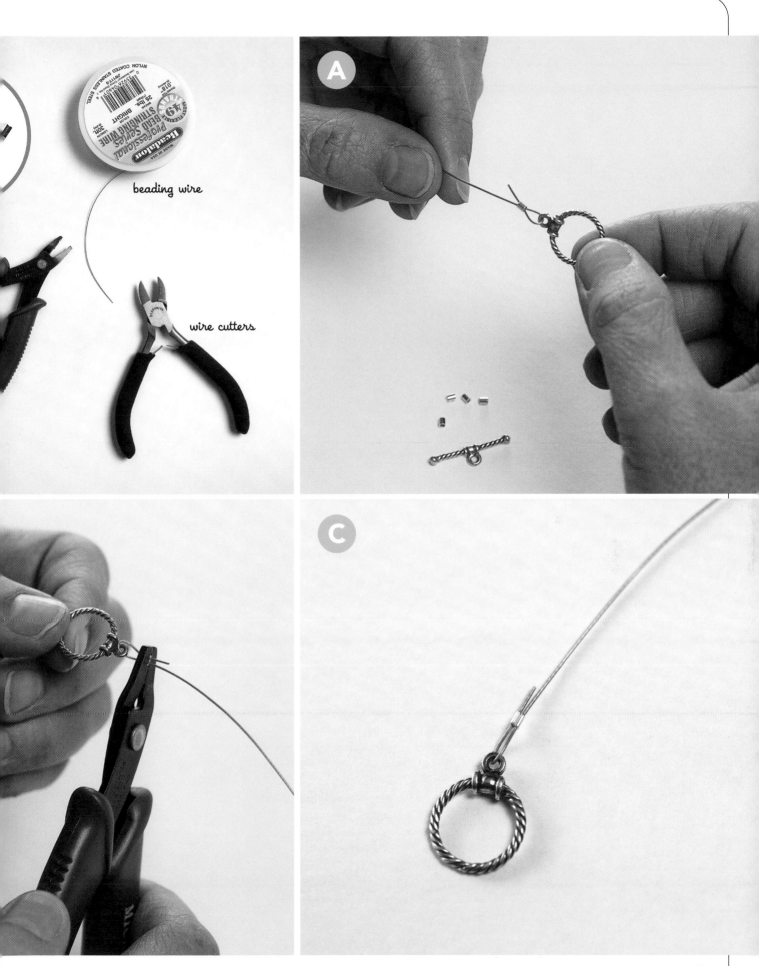

beading wire

wire cutters

A

C

glass bead-making supplies

Making glass beads seems intimidating, but with just a few tools and a little know-how, it's easy!

When making glass beads, keep safety in mind and read all instructions provided by the tool manufacturers. Gather these tools to make glass beads:

1 MAPP gas—an inexpensive flammable gas found in hardware stores.

2 Heatproof board—a fire-resistant stonelike piece on which to rest hot glass rods to prevent burning the work surface.

3 Bead separator—a thick pastelike substance used to coat the mandrel. This enables the bead to be removed from the mandrel when finished.

4 Vermiculite—can be used as a cooling substance. When the bead is finished, allow it to cool briefly until it starts to change color. Gently insert into vermiculite. This helps it to cool more slowly. Cooling the bead too fast in the open air will cause it to break. If vermiculite is unavailable use a warming blanket.

5 Glass rods—come in many different colors and can be solid, translucent, transparent, and dichroic (metallic coated). They range in price according to color and kind. The dichroic are the most expensive.

6 Mandrels—metal rods that come in different thicknesses. The thickness determines the size of hole in the bead. Those shown are dipped in bead separator, dried, and are ready to be used to form the glass. Mandrels can be reused.

7 Torch head for beadmaking—attachment made for beadmaking. Look for torch heads in the beading department of crafts and hobby stores.

8 Graphite paddle—a hard burnproof surface to roll a hot bead against to help shape it while it is still soft and pliable.

9 Striker—lights torches easily. Twist the valve on the tank to turn the gas on, hold the striker at the end of the torch head, and squeeze handle quickly to create a spark that ignites the torch.

10 Bead rake—a hook-like tool used for creating designs and altering the shape of hot glass.

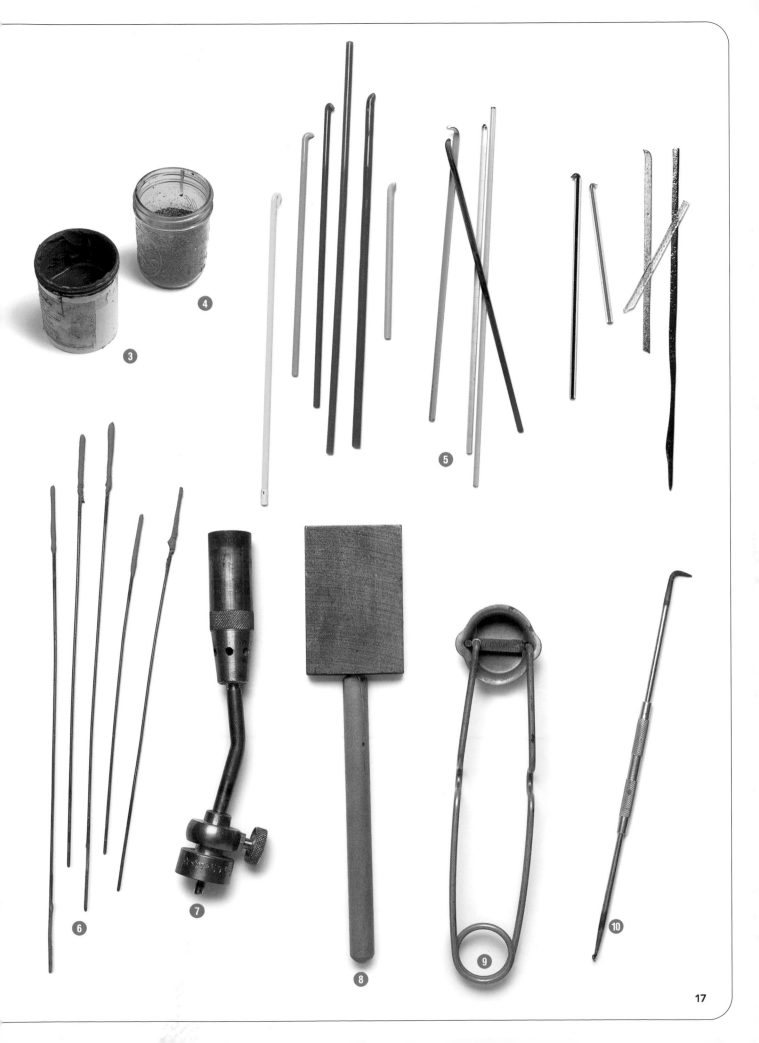

making glass beads

Now you have the tools ready—so it's time to be creative!

what you'll need

- Mandrels
- Bead separator
- Mapp gas
- Torch head for beadmaking
- Striker
- Glass rods
- Heatproof board
- Graphite paddle
- Vermiculite in a container

here's how

NOTE: Think safety first! Read the product directions before starting. Protect your work surface with a flame-retardant mat and wear eye goggles when using mapp gas. To protect your hands wear flame-retardant work gloves.

1. To prepare the mandrels dip each mandrel into the bead separator approximately 2–3 inches. Remove and let harden and dry well before using.
2. Light the torch with a striker.
3. Gradually warm a glass rod by moving it slowly into the heat beyond the end of the flame. Heating the rod too abruptly causes it to break. Continue to move the rod in and out of flame, gradually moving the rod to the tip of the flame where it is hottest as shown in Photo A. Slowly rotate the rod as it reddens and begins to melt until a red-hot ball begins to droop from the rod as shown in Photo B. Keep it in position at the tip of the flame.
4. With the other hand hold the prepared mandrel next to the glass rod, keeping the glass rod in the flame. Just when the mandrel turns red, move the glass rod to place the red-hot ball right on top of the red-hot mandrel. Slowly rotate the mandrel away from you while holding the glass rod steady until glass is completely rolled around the mandrel.
5. Keep the mandrel in the flame and gradually pull the glass rod away. Rest the hot glass rod on the heatproof board. Continue rotating the mandrel to keep the bead shape as even as possible.
6. Remove the bead from the flame quickly while still red and roll it onto the graphite paddle to smooth and shape it as shown in Photo C. Work quickly so bead stays hot.
7. Swiftly return bead to flame to smooth it out more if desired.
8. When the bead is finished, allow it to cool approximately 15 seconds until it begins to change color and then set it in a container of vermiculite as shown in Photo D. Shake some vermiculite over the bead until it is covered. Avoid stirring or pressing hard with mandrel. Allow bead to cool completely in vermiculite before removing.

making jewelry

Beads are created in every color
and shape—it's no wonder they're so
popular. This exciting chapter offers
inspiring ways to transform these timeless
treasures into wearable pieces of art.

timely
treasure

Make your watch even more fun to wear by beading the band in all your favorite colors and adding a cheery cherry charm.

what you'll need

1 mm elastic cord
Scissors; ruler
Watch face (purchase separately or remove the band from a watch)
Assortment of colored glass beads
Glue, such as E6000

here's how

❶ Cut three pieces of elastic, each approximately 10 inches long. The watch face shown has a small bar on each side where the band attaches. The width of the bar allows for several strands of beads. Tie the end of each elastic piece to the bar on one side, leaving a tail. Tie several knots until the elastic feels very secure. Thread several beads, tucking the tail back into the first few beads; trim off the excess elastic. Place a drop of glue on the knot. Let the glue dry.

❷ Continue stringing beads onto elastic randomly or by color if desired.

❸ After approximately 5 inches of beads are strung, loosely wrap the end of the elastic around the opposite watch bar. Test for fit, then add or remove beads. Finish other two strands in the same manner.

❹ With elastic stretched tie each end on the watch bar, knotting until firm. Tuck the end of elastic back into several beads, stretch, and trim off excess. Place a drop of glue on the knot. Let the glue dry.

birthday bracelets

Celebrate your birthday every day of the year by wearing this becoming birthstone-color bracelet.

what you'll need

2—2 mm sterling silver crimp beads
1—12-inch piece of .018-inch diameter stainless-steel beading wire
1—medium sterling silver toggle clasp
Crimping tool; wire cutters
6—4 mm seamless, smooth sterling silver beads
8—6 mm seamless, smooth sterling silver beads
10—4 mm sterling silver beaded rondelle spacer beads
4—5 mm sterling silver rondelle spacer beads
8—6 mm Swarovski square crystal beads in desired color to represent month (see page 111)
4—8 mm Swarovski square crystal beads in color above or birthstone color
To increase or decrease length, add or remove 5 mm sterling silver rondelle spacer beads and 4 mm seamless, smooth sterling silver beads.

here's how

1 Thread a crimp bead on one end of beading wire, pass wire through the end of toggle clasp, and run wire back through the crimp bead in the opposite direction. Flatten the crimp bead firmly. Trim the end.

2 Thread the beads in the following order:
3—4 mm smooth silver beads
1—6 mm smooth silver bead
1—4 mm silver rondelle spacer bead
1—6 mm square crystal bead
1—4 mm silver rondelle spacer bead
1—8 mm square crystal bead
1—4 mm silver rondelle spacer bead
1—6 mm square crystal bead
1—6 mm smooth silver bead
1—5 mm silver rondelle spacer bead
1—6 mm smooth silver bead
1—6 mm square crystal bead
1—4 mm silver rondelle spacer bead
1—8 mm square crystal bead
1—4 mm silver rondelle spacer bead
1—6 mm square crystal bead
1—6 mm smooth silver bead
1—5 mm silver rondelle spacer bead

Continue pattern until all the beads are used.

3 Thread a crimp bead on the end of the wire and pass it through the remaining clasp. Run wire back through crimp bead in opposite direction. Flatten crimp bead. Trim end.

for mother to love

Create a colorful variation of a birthday bracelet to represent all of your children's birthdays.

what you'll need

(This bracelet represents three children; adjust the crystal beads to fit your needs.)

2—2 mm sterling silver crimp beads
1—12-inch piece of .018 diameter stainless-steel beading wire
1—medium sterling silver toggle clasp
Crimping tool; wire cutters
12—4 mm seamless, smooth sterling silver beads
8—5 mm sterling silver beaded rondelle spacer beads
8—6 mm seamless, smooth sterling silver beads
4—4 mm sterling silver rondelle spacer beads
2—6 mm Swarovski square crystal beads in desired color to represent the first child's birth month (see page 111)
2—6 mm Swarovski square crystal beads in desired color to represent the second child's birth month
2—6 mm Swarovski square crystal beads in desired color to represent the third child's birth month
1—8 mm Swarovski square crystal bead in desired color to represent the first child's birth month
1—8 mm Swarovski square crystal bead in desired color to represent the second child's birth month
1—8 mm Swarovski square crystal bead in desired color to represent the third child's birth month
Jump ring

here's how

1 Thread a crimp bead on one end of beading wire, pass wire through the end of toggle clasp, and run wire back through the crimp bead in the opposite direction. Flatten the crimp bead firmly. Trim the end.

2 Decide on the beading pattern, keeping the number of children to be represented in mind. String the beads on the wire.

3 Thread a crimp bead on the end of the wire and pass it through the jump ring. Run the wire back through the crimp bead in the opposite direction. Flatten the crimp bead firmly. Trim the end.

cat's-eye chain

Make your specs spectacular with a happy holder threaded with cat's-eye beads.

what you'll need

1 yard of string or thread
32-inch strand of multicolor fiber-optic cat's-eye chips
2—3 mm crimp beads
36-inch piece of .019-inch diameter beading string
2 white eyeglass holder ends
Needle-nose pliers
Crimping tool; scissors

here's how

❶ Wrap string around neck to decide what length to make the eyeglasses holder, making it long enough to put on and take off easily. Cut the string to the desired length.

❷ If the 32-inch strand of cat's-eye chips are in a loop, carefully cut string. Lay the strand of chips on a flat work surface. Lay the string along side the strand. Pull off enough chips equally from each end to reach the desired length.

❸ Put a crimp bead on one end of the exposed strand and slide to about ¾ inch from the cat's-eye chips, being careful to avoid dropping chips off the other end. Pull the string through an eyeglass holder end. Pull string again through the crimp bead.

❹ Using needle-nose pliers, pull string until crimp bead is tight against the chips.

❺ Using crimping tool, crush crimp. Flip the string and crush crimp bead on other side. Clip off extra string.

❻ Repeat Steps 3–5 on the other end, attaching the string to the other eyeglasses holder end.

"I do" headpiece

The bride glows wearing this glistening headpiece as she steps down the aisle.

A

B

what you'll need

for the beaded ring

26-gauge silver wire; wire cutters
60—9×6 mm faceted oval crystal beads
120—5mm bicone crystal beads
5 yards of 6-inch-wide tulle; pins; hair comb
Needle-nose pliers; 26-gauge white wire

here's how

1 Cut the 26-gauge silver wire into fifty 12-inch lengths.

2 Place a faceted oval bead in the center of one 12-inch wire. Fold the wire down on each side. Twist bead to join the two pieces of wire together as in Diagram A, *opposite.* Spread the two wires apart. Make 12 wires beaded in this manner.

3 Place a bicone bead on one wire end. Pull the wires down around the sides of the bead and lay it at the bottom of the first twist. Twist the bead away from you; tightly twist about ½ inch. The twist should meet the twist from the first bead. Repeat on the right side.

4 Place the two end pieces of wire together to form a V as shown in Diagram B. Twist the beads to form a tight twist to the end of the wire. Repeat for all clusters.

5 Cut a 24-inch-long piece of silver wire and do the same three-bead formation as shown in Diagram C. Use this wire to start the wreath. Twist the 12-inch length of wire (use needle-nose pliers to fold and twist the length) and twist a cluster of beads on the right, ½ inch down from the first cluster. Wrap the 24-inch wire around the 12-inch wire. Form a third cluster under the second cluster to the left as shown in Diagram D.

6 When the 12-inch wire has 2 inches left, make another cluster of three beads on another 24-inch wire. Before you twist the two wires together, hook the 12-inch wire on a single cluster of beads on the wreath. Wrap it around wire on the wreath.

7 Continue until the desired length is achieved, approximately 11 or 12 inches.

8 Fold a 48-inch piece of wire in half. Place the fold around a cluster. Add clusters (one to the right, one to the left) until the wire is full.

9 Place the ring on head, overlapping both ends to decide length, and twist the ends tightly over each other. Attach a veil.

simple elegance

Lovely enough to grace a bride on her wedding day, this lustrous jewelry set sparkles with silver and crystal.

what you'll need

for the earrings

2—2-inch sterling silver headpins

2—4 mm sterling silver spacers

2—10 mm Swarovski square clear crystal beads

2—6 mm smooth round sterling silver beads

2—6 mm Swarovski square clear crystal beads

Wire cutters; needle-nose pliers

1 pair of medium to heavyweight sterling silver ear wires with ball and coil

here's how

❶ Thread beads on headpin as follows:

1—4 mm sterling silver spacer

1—10 mm Swarovski square clear crystal bead

1—6 mm sterling silver smooth round bead

1—6 mm Swarovski square clear crystal bead

❷ Clip end of headpin to ⅜ inch and bend at a 90-degree angle.

❸ Curve end into a loop using needle-nose pliers to form a uniform loop. Leave a small space open and attach to loop on ear wire. Close loop.

❹ Repeat Steps 1–3 for second earring.

for the necklace

2—2 mm sterling silver crimp beads

26-inch piece of .019-inch diameter
nylon-coated beading wire

6 mm spring ring clasp and jump ring

Crimping tool; wire cutters

72—3 mm smooth round silver beads

40—4 mm Swarovski square clear crystal beads

30—4–6 mm sterling silver beaded spacer beads

18—6 mm Swarovski square clear crystal beads

12—6 mm smooth round sterling silver beads

1—10 mm Swarovski square clear crystal bead

here's how

1 Thread a crimp bead on one end of the wire, pass it through the end of the spring ring clasp, and run the wire back through the crimp bead in the opposite direction. Flatten the crimp bead firmly. Trim the end.

2 Thread the beads in the following order:

  20—3 mm round silver beads

Alternate 1—4 mm square crystal bead with 3mm round silver bead seven times.

Alternate three times:

  1—4 mm square crystal bead

  1—4–6 mm sterling spacer

  1—6 mm square crystal bead

  1—4–6 mm sterling spacer

  1—4 mm square crystal bead

  1—6 mm round sterling silver bead

Then string 1—4mm square crystal bead.

Alternate three times:

  1—4–6 mm sterling silver spacer

  1—6 mm square crystal bead

  1—4–6 mm sterling spacer bead

  1—6 mm round sterling silver bead

  1—4–6 sterling spacer bead

  1—4 mm square crystal bead

  1—3 mm round silver bead

  1—6 mm square crystal bead

  1—3 mm round silver bead

  1—4 mm square crystal bead

  1—3 mm round silver bead

Then string 1—10 mm square crystal bead and reverse the order, starting with the 3 mm round silver bead and ending with the 20—3 mm round silver beads.

3 Thread a crimp bead on the end and pass the wire through the jump ring. Run the wire back through the crimp bead in the opposite direction. Flatten the crimp bead firmly. Trim the excess wire.

for the bracelet

2—2 mm sterling silver crimp beads

10 to12-inch piece of .018-inch diameter
stainless-steel beading wire

6 mm spring ring clasp and jump ring

Crimping tool; wire cutters

20—3 mm smooth round silver beads

12—4 mm Swarovski square clear
crystal beads

7—6mm Swarovski square clear crystal beads

here's how

1 Thread a crimp bead on one end of the wire, pass it through the end of the spring ring clasp, and run the wire back through the crimp bead in the opposite direction. Flatten the crimp bead firmly. Trim the end.

2 Thread on the beads in the following order:

  6—3 mm round silver beads

  1—4 mm square crystal bead

  1—3 mm round silver bead

  1—4 mm square crystal bead

  1—3 mm round silver bead

  1—4 mm square crystal bead

  1—6 mm square crystal bead

  1—4 mm Square crystal bead

  1—3 mm round silver bead

  1—4 mm square crystal bead

  1—6 mm square crystal bead

  1—4 mm square crystal bead

  1—3 mm round silver bead

  1—6 mm square crystal bead

Add one more 6 mm square crystal bead and finish the bracelet, reversing the order of the beads listed above.

3 Thread a crimp bead on the end and pass the wire through the jump ring. Run the wire back through the crimp bead in the opposite direction. Flatten the crimp bead firmly. Trim the excess wire.

love loops

Choose pewter or glass charms to personalize strings of beads and wear them on your favorite jeans!

what you'll need

1—30-inch piece of .019 diameter micro stainless-steel nylon-coated beading wire
Wire cutters
1- or 1½-inch key ring with flexible chain and jump ring
6—2 mm crimp beads; crimping tool

for the teal loop

3 pewter charms
70—3 mm teal and green glass beads
3—6 mm blue glass beads
10 vintage teal and green beads, ceramic or wood
6—6 mm lime green miracle beads
7—tube silver-plated spacer beads
3—saucer silver-plated spacer beads
2—6 mm round blue-green crystal beads
1—16 mm rectangular blue-green glass bead
1—10 mm teardrop lime green crystal bead

for the red loop

2 pewter charms
1 large heart-shape red glass bead
4—3 mm dark gray glass beads
6—4 mm red miracle or vintage beads
5—8 mm disk-shape red crystal beads
13—3 mm dark red glass beads
3—3 mm diamond-shape dark red crystal beads
6—8 mm diamond-shape dark red beads
4—cone-shape red vintage beads
1—8 mm round dark red glass bead
1—8 mm oblong red vintage bead
2—10 to16 mm oblong red glass or crystal beads
8—5×3 mm tube Hemalyke (synthetic hematite) beads
6—7×5 mm rectangular Hemalyke beads
3 ornate tube silver-plated spacer beads
4 ornate round silver-plated spacer beads

here's how

❶ Cut three 10-inch pieces of beading wire. Fold one wire in half. Place the fold through the center of the key ring, bring the ends up through the loop, and pull tight.
❷ Thread the beads on the wires in the desired order.
❸ Thread a crimp bead on one end and pass the wires though a charm or large bead. Thread the wires back through the crimp bead in the opposite direction. Flatten the crimp bead firmly. Trim the ends.
❹ Repeat Steps 1–4 for the remaining wires.

hinged ear wires
instructions on page 35

last-minute hoops
instructions on page 36

jewel drop earrings
instructions on page 36

teardrop ear studs
instructions on page 37

pendant earrings
instructions on page 37

vintage clip-ons
instructions on page 3

black bangles
instructions on page 36

Hemalyke earrings
instructions on page 37

candy cane earrings
instructions on page 38

earrings with style

Whichever look you choose, these earrings work up so quickly, you'll want a pair in every color of the rainbow.

what you'll need

for the hinged ear wires

2—3-inch-long, .021-inch diameter headpins
4—3 mm sterling silver saucer spacer beads
2—16×12 mm 3-sided peach glass beads
2—4 mm corrugated sterling silver saucer spacer beads
2—10×8 mm oval peach glass beads
Wire cutters; needle-nose pliers
1 pair of hinged ear wires

here's how

❶ For each earring thread beads on a headpin in the following order:
1—3 mm sterling silver saucer spacer bead
1—16×12 mm three-sided peach glass bead
1—4 mm corrugated saucer spacer bead
1—10×8 mm oval peach glass bead
1—3 mm sterling silver saucer spacer bead
❷ Clip the end of the headpin to ⅜ inch and bend at a 90-degree angle.
❸ Curve the end into a uniform loop using needle-nose pliers; leave a small space open to attach loop to hinged ear wire. Attach loop to wire; close loop.

continued on page 36

what you'll need

for the last-minute hoops

1 pair of 1-inch (or desired size) round sterling silver beading hoops

4—6 mm round sterling silver beads

2—10–12 mm matching rainbow candy cane glass beads

here's how

❶ For each earring, open the hoop and slide on one 6 mm round sterling silver bead. Slide on one rainbow candy cane glass bead and another 6 mm sterling silver bead.

what you'll need

for the black bangles

2—2-inch-long sterling silver headpins

2—2 mm round sterling silver beads

2—oval iridescent black glass beads

2—3 mm diamond-shape clear crystal beads

Wire cutters; needle-nose pliers

1 pair of medium to heavyweight sterling silver ear wires with ball and coil

here's how

❶ Thread beads on headpin in the following order:

    1—2mm round sterling silver bead

    1—oval iridescent black glass bead

    1—3mm diamond-shape clear crystal bead

❷ Clip end of headpin to ⅜ inch and bend at a 90-degree angle.

❸ Curve end into a loop using needle-nose pliers to form a uniform circle. Leave a small space open and attach to loop on ear wire. Close circle.

❹ Repeat Steps 1–3 for second earring.

what you'll need

for the jewel drop earrings

2—3-inch-long sterling silver headpins

4—4 mm sterling silver beaded spacer beads

4—3 mm diamond-shape blue crystal bead

2—6 mm diamond-shape clear crystal bead

Wire cutters; needle-nose pliers

1 pair of medium-weight sterling silver ear wires with coil and 5 mm silver beaded ball

here's how

❶ Thread beads on headpin as follows:

    1—4 mm sterling silver beaded spacer bead

    1—3 mm diamond-shape blue crystal bead

    1—6 mm diamond-shape clear crystal bead

    1—4 mm sterling silver beaded spacer bead

❷ Clip end of headpin to ⅜ inch and bend at a 90-degree angle.

❸ Curve end into a loop using needle-nose pliers to form a uniform circle. Leave a small space open and attach to loop underneath silver beaded ball on ear wire. Close circle.

❹ Repeat Steps 1–3 for second earring.

what you'll need

for the teardrop ear studs
2—2-inch-long, .021-inch diameter headpins
4—3 mm sterling silver beaded spacer beads
2—10 mm teardrop pink crystal beads
2—6 mm smooth sterling silver beads
wire cutters; needle-nose pliers
1 pair—4 mm sterling silver ear studs

here's how

1 For each earring thread beads on a headpin in the following order:
    1—3 mm sterling silver beaded spacer bead
    1—10 mm teardrop pink crystal
    1—6 mm smooth sterling silver bead
    1—3 mm sterling silver beaded spacer bead
2 Clip the end of the headpin to ⅜ inch and bend at a 90-degree angle.
3 Curve the end into a uniform loop using needle-nose pliers; leave a small space open to attach to loop below ball on post. Close the loop.

what you'll need

for the Hemalyke earrings
1 pair—24-gauge sterling silver curved-back kidney ear wires
2—2-inch-long, .021-inch-diameter headpins
4—4 mm corrugated sterling silver saucer spacer beads
2—3 mm Hemalyke (synthetic hematite)

rondelle beads
2—6×4 mm Hemalyke tube beads
2—3 mm corrugated sterling silver saucer spacer beads
Wire cutters; needle-nose pliers

here's how

1 For each earring thread beads on a headpin in the following order:
    1—4 mm sterling silver saucer spacer bead
    1—3 mm Hemalyke rondelle bead
    1—4 mm sterling silver saucer spacer bead
    1—6×4mm Hemalyke tube bead
    1—3 mm sterling silver saucer spacer beads
2 Clip the end of the headpin to ⅜ inch and bend at a 90-degree angle.
3 Curve the end into a loop using needle-nose pliers to form a uniform circle. Leave a small space open and attach loop to kidney ear wire. Close circle.

what you'll need

for the pendant earrings
2—sterling silver jump rings
Needle-nose pliers
2—pendants
2—sterling silver post earrings

here's how

1 For each earring, slightly open the jump ring using needle-nose pliers.
2 Attach the teardrop pendant and post to the jump ring.
3 Close the opening in the jump ring.

continued on page 38

what you'll need

for the vintage clip-ons

2—sterling silver headpins
2—4 mm clear glass beads
2—20 mm green vintage glass beads
2—6 mm clear glass beads
2—3 mm green glass beads
Wire cutters; needle-nose pliers
1 pair—hinged sterling silver clip-on earrings

here's how

1 Thread beads on headpin in the following order:
   1—4 mm clear glass bead
   1—20 mm green vintage glass bead
   1—6 mm clear glass bead
   1—3 mm green glass bead
2 Clip end of headpin to ⅜ inch and bend at a 90-degree angle.
3 Curve the end into a loop using needle-nose pliers to form a uniform circle. Leave a small space open and attach to loop on front of hinged silver clip-on earring. Close circle.
4 Repeat Steps 1–3 for second earring.

what you'll need

for the candy cane earings

2—3-inch-long, .021-inch-diameter sterling silver headpins
4—4 mm blue glass spacer beads
4—4 mm lime green glass spacer beads
2 matching 10 mm cylinder shape candy cane glass beads
Wire cutters; needle-nose pliers
1 pair of medium to heavyweight sterling silver ear wires with ball and coil

here's how

1 For each earring thread beads on a headpin in the following order:
   1—4 mm blue glass spacer
   1—4 mm lime green glass spacer
   1—10 mm cylinder-shape candy cane glass bead
   1—4 mm lime green glass spacer
   1—4 mm blue glass spacer
2 Clip the end of the headpin to ⅜ inch and bend at a 90-degree angle.
3 Curve the end into a uniform loop using needle-nose pliers. Leave a small space open and attach to loop on front of ear wire. Close circle.Attach to ear wire.

doll
necklace

Girls of all ages will love this sweet doll necklace that has a heart bead for a skirt.

what you'll need

30-gauge brass wire; wire cutters
1—¾-inch heart-shape bead
Seed beads and bugle beads for arms and
    legs; small butterfly bead
Needle-nose pliers
1 petal-shape silver sequin
1 round silver bead for head

here's how

➊ Cut five 6-inch lengths of wire.
➋ Place the heart bead upside down and thread four of the wires up through the heart. Center the heart on the wires.
➌ For the legs divide the wire into two groups. Thread 11 seed beads onto each leg. Place one bugle bead and finish with one seed bead. Cut off excess wire ½ inch from the last bead. Use needle-nose pliers to twist the remaining ½ inch into a loop. Bend bugle bead up to form a foot.
➍ Slip the four wires on top through the petal sequin, a seed bead, and the round silver bead.
➎ Bend down two of the wires to form a loop. Twist them together several times. Use needle-nose pliers to form curls from the ends of these two wires. Curl the remaining two wires with the pliers.
➏ For the arms slip the fifth wire under the sequin and twist it several times around the neck. Thread on three seed beads, one bugle bead, and three more seed beads. Finish the end with a loop of wire as for the legs. On the second arm omit the last seed bead and thread on a butterfly bead.
➐ Use fingers to fold the sequin collar in half so it lies flat against the body.

string
of elegance

Adorned in ocean tones of blue and green, this necklace features an elegant trio of beaded strands.

what you'll need

71 inches 26 lb. nylon-covered wire
8—silver crimp beads; crimping tool
Claw hook or trigger clasp and ring fastener
18—4 mm round turquoise beads
5—8 mm green beads in assorted shapes
6—8 mm light blue beads in assorted shapes
3—8 mm turquoise beads in assorted shapes
297 dark blue bugle beads
4—8 mm flat white beads; wire cutters

here's how

1 Cut three wires each 23½ inches long.
2 String one wire through a crimp bead, then through hole in claw hook, and back through crimp bead, leaving ⅜ inch wire at the end to cut off when necklace is complete. Position crimp bead close to claw without touching. Squeeze crimp bead tight over both wires.
3 String a second crimp bead on same wire. Insert ends of two other wires into same crimp bead, positioning bead next to first crimp bead. Squeeze crimp bead over all three wires.
4 String nine round turquoise beads over all three strands. Thread all three strands through a crimp bead and squeeze shut.
5 Separate one strand and thread through one crimp bead. Position close to other crimp bead and squeeze tightly shut.
6 Bead each string with blue bugle beads. When 5 inches of beads are strung, thread assorted color beads periodically about an inch apart with blue tube beads between. Make each strand 17½ inches long.
7 Combine necklace into one strand at this point. String strand with crimp bead through another crimp bead and crimp shut where blue tube beads end.
8 Thread all three wires through another crimp bead and crimp over all three strands.
9 Thread nine turquoise beads on all three strands. Thread all three wires through a crimp bead and squeeze tightly shut.
10 Cut two wires off close to crimp bead, leaving third wire long.
11 Thread remaining wire through a crimp bead, through ring fastener, and back through the same crimp bead. Position crimp bead close to beads and close to ring fastener without touching. Squeeze crimp bead tightly. Cut extra wire off each end. Tuck ends inside closest bead to hide.

seeded
beads

Black, white, and silver beads make a striking earring and bracelet set.

what you'll need

Silver seed beads
Waxed paper; large paper clip
Oven-bake clay, such as Sculpey, in black and
    pearl white
Large paper clip; glass baking dish
Large black seed beads
Wire cutters
22-gauge silver wire
Needle-nose pliers; earring wires
2—½-inch flat silver beads
Scissors; beading elastic

here's how

1 To make clay black beads, place silver seed beads on a piece of waxed paper. Shape 10 small balls (slightly larger than a pea) from black clay. Roll each clay ball in beads, allowing the silver beads to stick randomly in clay as shown in Photo A, *left*. Gently poke a hole in the center of each bead with an opened paper clip as shown in Photo B; move the clip in a small circular motion to enlarge the opening. Set finished clay beads on baking dish.

2 To make the white beads, shape 10 balls from white clay. Slightly flatten each bead. Press a black seed bead in the center of each flattened side. Gently poke a hole in each bead's center at the narrow edge; move the paper clip in a small circular motion to enlarge the opening. Set beads on baking dish.

3 Bake the beads in the oven according to the manufacturer's instructions. Let cool.

4 *To make the earrings* cut two 2-inch-long pieces of silver wire. Using pliers make a tiny loop in one end, placing on the earring wire before closing. Thread a white, flat silver, and black bead on each wire. Thread on three silver seed beads. Clip wire ends, leaving ¼ inch at each end. Use pliers to shape a spiral at each wire end.

5 *To make a bracelet* cut a piece of beading elastic 4 inches longer than desired length. Thread clay beads on elastic, alternating the colors. Before knotting the elastic ends, check the fit. Add or remove beads for fit. Knot ends; trim excess.

beaded black bracelet

wire-wrapped
circles bracelet

wonderfully wired

wild wire bracelet

Accent store-bought rubber rings with brilliant crafting wire to make jewelry with eclectic flair.

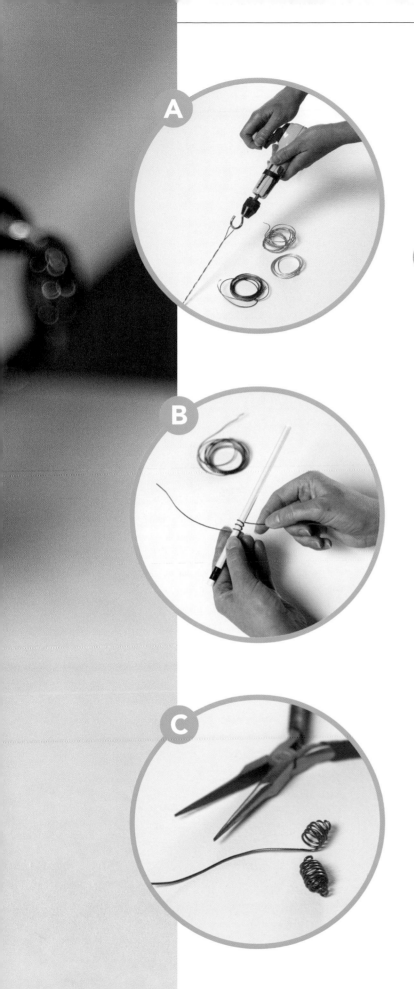

wild wire bracelet

what you'll need

for wild wire bracelet

18-gauge metallic or plastic-covered wire in blue, red, yellow, green, and purple
Wire cutters; hand drill; cup hooks; tape
Needle-nose pliers; round pencil
5—⅜-inch O rings (available in hardware and home supply stores); round toothpick

here's how

1 To make a blue S bead, cut a 12-inch piece of wire; fold it in half. Place the cup hook in the drill as a bit. Place the wire loop over the hook. Tape wire ends to a work surface; crank the drill handle as shown in Photo A, *left.* Use pliers to shape ends into coils that form an S.

2 To make a red loop bead, cut a 5-inch length of wire. Wrap the center of the wire around a round pencil three times; remove from pencil. Gently pull loops slightly apart and flatten. Form wire ends into open loops.

3 To make a twisted yellow bead, cut a 12-inch piece of wire. Fold it in half. Place the fold of the wire in the drill; turn to twist. Wrap the center of the wire around a round pencil five times; remove. Gently pull loops apart. Use pliers to tuck wire ends into bead center.

4 To make a green bead, cut a 4-inch length of wire. Wrap around a toothpick to shape.

5 To make a purple spiral bead, cut a 10-inch length of wire. Wrap the wire around a pencil three times as shown in Photo B. Use pliers to shape the ends into loops as in Photo C.

6 Cut short pieces of red wire to attach the beads to the O rings. *NOTE: For the yellow, green, and purple beads, the red wire is threaded through the bead before the end loops are shaped. To attach the S bead, shape red wire into O shapes.* Pinch the wire end loops closed with pliers.

continued on page 46

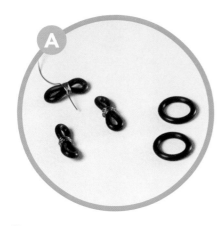

A

what you'll need

for beaded black bracelet
26-gauge blue metallic wire
Wire cutter
Approximately five $^7/_{16}$-inch O rings
Needle-nose pliers
Golden beading wire
Approximately five $^3/_8$-inch O rings
Large iridescent black seed beads
Golden bead

here's how

1 Cut five 3-inch lengths of 26-gauge blue metallic wire. Bend a $^7/_{16}$-inch O ring in half. Wind the center of the O ring tightly with wire as shown in Photo A, *above*. Use pliers to pinch down the wire ends.

2 Cut five 12-inch lengths of golden beading wire. Fold wire in half. To join the $^7/_{16}$-inch and $^3/_8$-inch rings, thread the wire loop through one end of the $^7/_{16}$-inch O ring. Thread the ends through the loop and tighten to secure. Wrap the wires around both rings several times. Thread three seed beads on wire. Join the $^3/_8$-inch ring to another $^7/_{16}$-inch ring as before, threading the loose ends back through the beads. Cut the wire if needed.

3 Try on the bracelet. Add or remove O rings to fit. For closure string a golden bead and seed bead on the end of the bracelet, opposite a $^7/_{16}$-inch ring.

what you'll need

for wire-wrapped circles bracelet
Wire cutters
18-gauge wire in chartreuse and purple
22-gauge copper wire
Approximately eleven $^7/_{16}$-inch O rings
Needle-nose pliers

here's how

1 Cut 4-inch lengths of wire, six from 18-gauge wire and four from 22-gauge wire.

2 To join O rings stack two together. Thread one 4-inch length of wire through the rings. Centering the wire wrap it around the rings twice as shown in Photo A, *below*. Trim each wire end to 1 inch. Gently pull the rings apart to lie flat.

3 Use needle-nose pliers to bend the wire ends into spirals as shown in Photo B.

4 Continue linking O rings until the desired bracelet length is achieved.

5 Before attaching the closure try on the bracelet. Add or remove beads to fit. To make a closure cut a 2-inch-long piece of 18-gauge wire. Fold it in half. Shape the open ends into a ring, closing it around one end O ring. Use pliers to fold the other end into a hook.

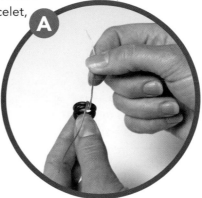

A

B

little angels bracelet

Choose jeweled boy and girl charms to signify the special little ones in your life.

what you'll need

Assortment of colorful glass beads
Variety of golden or silver spacer beads
Boy and/or girl charms
1 mm elastic beading cord
Scissors; tape
Glue, such as E6000

here's how

❶ For a bracelet, plan a length of beads approximately 7 inches long. Use golden or silver spacer beads between the glass beads, inserting charms where desired.

❷ Cut a 12-inch length of elastic. Tape one end down onto work surface. String on the beads. Untape the elastic from the work surface and check the size on wrist. Add or remove beads if necessary to fit wrist.

❸ Stretch the elastic and tie a knot. Avoid overstretching or beads may pucker. Tie several more knots until secure and trim off excess elastic.

❹ Add a dot of glue to the knot. Let the glue dry.

awareness bracelets

Design heartwarming bracelets in a color theme to pique awareness or raise funds for a worthwhile cause.

2—2 mm sterling silver crimp beads
Crimping tool; 10- to12-inch piece of .018
   diameter stainless-steel beading wire
1 medium sterling silver lobster clasp and
   jump ring
10—2.5 mm smooth, seamless sterling silver
   beads; wire cutters
6—3 mm diamond-shape crystal beads in
   color to represent organization
4—4 mm sterling silver beaded rondelle
   spacer beads
12—6 mm cat's-eye beads in color to match
6—5 mm sterling silver beaded rondelle
   spacer beads
4—6 mm rhinestone rondelle spacer beads
1—8 mm crystal bead

here's how

❶ Thread a crimp bead on one end of the
beading wire and pass wire through the end of
the lobster clasp. Run wire back through the
crimp bead in the opposite direction. Flatten
the crimp bead firmly. Trim wire end.
❷ Thread the beads in the following order:
  3—2.5 mm silver beads
  1—3 mm diamond-shape crystal bead
  1—2.5 mm silver bead
  1—3 mm diamond-shape crystal bead
  1—2.5 mm silver bead
  1—3 mm diamond-shape crystal bead
  1—4 mm silver beaded spacer bead
  1—6 mm cat's-eye bead
  1—5 mm silver spacer bead
  1—6 mm cat's-eye bead
  1—6 mm rhinestone spacer bead
  1—6 mm cat's-eye bead
  1—5 mm silver beaded spacer bead
  1—6 mm cat's-eye bead
  1—6 mm rhinestone spacer bead
  1—6 mm cat's-eye bead
  1—5 mm silver beaded spacer bead
  1—6 mm cat's-eye bead
  1—4 mm silver beaded spacer bead
  1—8 mm crystal bead
After the 8 mm crystal bead is threaded,
continue threading the beads in reverse order
starting with the 4 mm beaded spacer.
❸ Thread a crimp bead on the end and pass
the wire through the jump ring. Run the wire
back through the crimp bead in the opposite
direction. Flatten crimp bead. Trim the end.

you name it

Show pride in your children or any loved ones by wearing their names on your wrist.

what you'll need

Assorted sterling silver beads and spacers
28 black hematite beads; wire cutters
4 mm square sterling silver letter beads
2—2-hole spacers (small metal rods with 2 holes)
24 inches of 26 lb. nylon-covered wire
Wire cutters
4—2 mm sterling silver crimp beads
Claw hook or trigger clasp and ring fastener
Crimping tool

here's how

1 Measure wrist for desired length. The recommended length is 7 or 7½ inches. Lay out beads in pattern before beginning to string. Pattern in bracelet shown alternates silver beads with black hematite beads before the name begins; then a silver bead alternates with a letter bead. Use two-hole spacers before and after letter beads to connect the strands together in a two-strand bracelet.

2 Cut two 12-inch-long pieces of wire.

3 String one wire through a crimp bead, through hole in claw hook, and back through crimp bead, leaving ⅜ inch wire hanging at the end. Position crimp bead close to claw without touching. Squeeze the crimp bead tightly over both wires.

4 String second wire through a crimp bead, through hole in same claw hook, and back through crimp bead following same instructions as in Step 3. Squeeze crimp bead tightly over both wires so there are two wires attached to one fastener.

5 Begin stringing the first string with beads in the planned pattern. Add a two-hole spacer before first letter and after the last letter.

6 Copy the beading pattern on second string. Thread wire through hole in each two-hole spacer where it is hanging. Use an extra bead or two if the number of letters in each name is different so the 2-hole spacer is straight between both strands. Continue placing beads until bracelet is complete.

7 Check that each strand is same length. Add a crimp bead to the first string. Place crimp bead close to fastener without touching it and squeeze tightly. Finish remaining string same way.

8 Cut off extra wire ends close to beads and hide the ends inside the closest bead.

a barrel of fun

Vibrant barrel beads are linked by small beads to form a playful chain bracelet.

what you'll need

7–10 glass barrel beads
30-inch piece of elastic cord
80–110—5 mm round colored glass beads
Scissors

here's how

1 Slide a barrel bead to the middle of the elastic piece as shown in Diagram A, *below.*
2 String five 5 mm beads on each end of the elastic as shown in Diagram B. Thread the ends through another barrel bead from opposite directions as shown in Diagram C.
3 Continue threading beads in this manner until the desired bracelet length is achieved. Thread the elastic ends through the first barrel bead in the same manner.
4 Knot the elastic ends securely. Thread the elastic ends back through several beads and trim the excess.

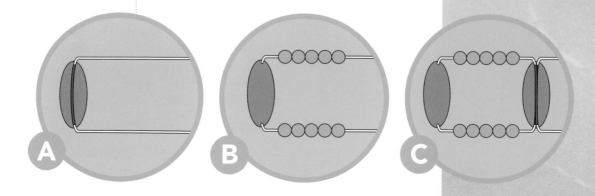

A   B   C

falling leaves
lariat

String a long wire to double up as a distinctive necklace style. You can make one for every season by changing the color scheme.

what you'll need

Beading wire
Wire cutters
Seed beads
4 leaf-shape beads
Assorted beads
Tape
Needle-nose pliers

here's how

1 Cut two 100-inch strands of beading wire.

2 String a seed bead onto one end of wire, leaving a 4-inch tail.

3 Thread on a leaf bead.

4 Pull the 4-inch wire tail through the leaf bead, tightening the seed bead against the leaf bead.

5 Continue stringing assorted beads onto the wire, hiding the wire tail within the beads. String 3 inches of the wire using the desired combination of seed and assorted beads.

6 Repeat Steps 2–5 with the other wire, stringing 6 inches with beads.

7 Begin stringing seed beads onto one wire. If desired create a pattern by using other assorted beads. String approximately 48 inches of beads.

8 Tape loose end of wire onto surface to keep beads from slipping off.

9 Take other strand of partially strung wire and push loose wire end into the beads on the first strand, beginning at the seed beads. Thread wire through all of the beads and pull snugly to eliminate any space between the beads.

10 Finish both tails as in Steps 2–6, reversing the general order of the beads and varying the length of each tail.

11 After placing the leaf and seed beads, use pliers to pull wire back through the leaf bead and several other beads in the necklace.

12 To wear fold the beaded wire in half as shown in Diagram A, *left*. Place beads around neck and bring the ends through the loop as shown in Diagram B. Adjust as desired.

A

B

roll out the pendants

Embed intricately detailed clay pendants with a hint of shiny metal. For more designs, turn to pages 58-61.

ball chain design

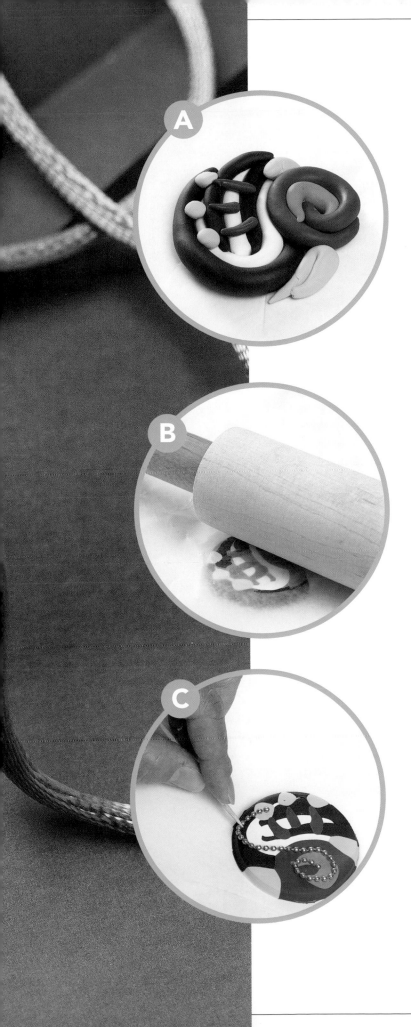

for the ball chain design

Polymer clay in pink, white, purple, aqua,
   and black
Waxed paper
Rolling pin
Lid in desired pendant size
Baking dish
2-inch piece of silver ball chain
Toothpick
Clear acrylic sealer and paintbrush, optional
34 inches of pink satin cord

here's how

① Shape small coils from each color of clay.
Using Photo A, *left*, for inspiration, bend and
arrange the coils in a circular shape on waxed
paper. Add small balls of aqua. Place waxed
paper over the clay and roll it until it is about
3/8 inch thick as shown in Photo B.

② Remove the waxed paper. Using the lid as
a cookie cutter, cut pendant from clay.
Remove the lid. Remove the excess clay from
around the edge of the circle. Place the clay
on a baking dish.

③ Lay the ball chain on the clay and arrange
it to follow part of the design in the clay. Use
a toothpick to push the chain into the clay as
shown in Photo C.

④ Roll two clay ropes approximately 6 inches
long, one from pink and one from black. Place
the two ropes together, hold one end, and
twist the colors to make a two-tone rope.
Shape the rope around the clay circle. Shape
one end into a spiral for a hanging loop. Bake
the clay in the oven according to the clay
manufacturer's directions. Let cool.

⑤ If desired paint the clay piece with a clear
acrylic sealer and let dry.

⑥ Fold cord in half. Push the fold through
the loop in the pendant. Thread the cord ends
through the loop in the cord and tighten.
Knot the cord ends to wear.

continued on page 58

57

abstract pendant

what you'll need

for the abstract pendant

Polymer clay in black, royal blue, green, red,
and yellow
Waxed paper; rolling pin
Lid in desired pendant size; baking dish
Large silver eyelet; 3 green eyelets
Needle-nose pliers; toothpick
1-inch piece of silver solder; 1 black eyelet
Clear acrylic sealer and paintbrush, optional
34-inch length of suede lacing
Silver bead with large hole
Baking dish

floral pendant

here's how

1 Roll grape-size pieces of black and royal
blue clay into a ball. Place the ball on waxed
paper and place another sheet on top of the
clay. Use a rolling pin to flatten the clay until it
is about ¼ inch thick.

2 Remove the waxed paper. Using the lid as a
cookie cutter, cut pendant from clay. Remove
the lid. Remove the excess clay from around
the edge of the circle. Roll three tiny clay ropes
from green and one from red. Shape as desired
and place on circle. Roll two small balls and
shape one flat square from yellow and place on
circle. Place waxed paper over the design and
gently roll with a rolling pin. Remove the waxed
paper and place the clay on a baking dish.

3 Use a toothpick to press green and silver
eyelets into the clay. Form a small red clay ball
and press in the center of the silver eyelet. Use
needle-nose pliers to shape solder into a coil
and press into the clay.

4 Roll two clay ropes approximately 6 inches
long, one from black and one from royal blue.
Place the two ropes together, hold one end,
and twist the colors to make a two-tone rope.
Roll on flat surface until smooth. Shape the
smooth rope around the clay circle; trim excess.
Use fingers scallop edge every ½ inch. Use a
toothpick to make a small hole for hanging;
insert a black eyelet. Bake the clay in the oven
according to the clay manufacturer's directions.

5 If desired, paint the clay piece with a clear
acrylic sealer and let dry.

6 Thread suede lacing through the black
eyelet. Slip silver bead over both ends of lacing
and snug to pendant. Knot the lacing ends.

what you'll need

for the floral pendant

Polymer clay in white, purple, red, yellow, and
green; rolling pin; waxed paper
Blue flower eyelet; needle-nose pliers
Lid in desired pendant size
Clear sealer and paintbrush, optional
34-inch length of plastic cording; baking dish

here's how

1 Roll grape-size pieces of white clay into a
ball. Place the ball on waxed paper and place
another sheet on top of the clay. Use a rolling
pin to flatten the clay to a ¼-inch-thick circle.

2 Make a rope from purple clay. Wrap rope
around white clay. Place waxed paper on top
of clay and flatten slightly.

3 Remove the waxed paper. Using the lid as
a cookie cutter, cut pendant from clay.
Remove the lid. Remove the excess clay from
around the edge of the circle.

4 Shape two small leaves from green clay;
press onto pendant. Roll a long narrow coil
from red clay. Shape into loops and press into
the center of the pendant.

5 Roll a small ball from yellow clay; flatten.
Use scissors to fringe the edge. Press onto the
pendant using a flower eyelet in the center.

6 Roll short coils from red and yellow; twist
together. Make a loop in the center and press
each end onto the top of the pendant.

7 Bake clay in oven according to the
manufacturer's directions. If desired paint the
clay piece with clear sealer; let dry. Thread
cording through the loop; knot cording ends.

continued on page 60

59

garden pendant

what you'll need

for the garden pendant

Polymer clay in light blue, yellow, green, pink,
 and white; waxed paper; rolling pin
Lid in desired pendant size; baking dish
Red heart-shape and round eyelets
Floral eyelets in orange and blue
Clear acrylic sealer and paintbrush, optional
36-inch length of red plastic cording

here's how

1 Roll one-quarter of a light blue clay square
into a ball. Place the ball on waxed paper and
place another sheet on top of the clay. Use a
rolling pin to flatten the clay until it is about ¼
inch thick.
2 Remove the waxed paper. Using the lid as
a cookie cutter, cut pendant from clay.
Remove lid. Remove excess clay from around
edge of circle. Place the clay on a baking dish.
3 Roll two long clay ropes approximately
6 inches long, one from yellow and one from
light blue. Place the ropes together, hold one
end, and twist the colors to make a two-tone
rope. Shape the rope around the clay circle.
Shape the ends into a spiral for hanging.
4 Shape stems and leaves from green clay.
Roll tiny clay balls for flower centers. Place
clay pieces on pendant and press eyelets over
centers. Bake the clay in the oven according
to the clay manufacturer's directions.
5 If desired paint the clay piece with a clear
acrylic sealer; let dry. Thread the cord through
the loop at the top of the pendant.

what you'll need

for the eyelet hearts pendant

Polymer clay in black and white
Waxed paper; rolling pin
Lid in desired pendant size; baking dish
Toothpick
Heart-shape eyelets in 5 colors
Clear acrylic sealer and paintbrush, optional
36-inch length of black leather lacing
2—8 mm clear glass beads

here's how

1 Roll one-quarter of a black clay square
into a ball. Place the ball on waxed paper and
place another sheet on top of the clay. Use a
rolling pin to flatten the clay until it is about
¼ inch thick.
2 Remove the waxed paper. Using the lid as
a cookie cutter, cut pendant from clay as
shown in Photo A, *opposite*. Remove the lid.
Remove the excess clay from around the edge
of the circle. Place the clay on a baking dish.
3 Use a toothpick to press eyelets into the
clay in a circular design as shown in Photo B.
4 Roll two clay ropes approximately 6 inches
long, one from white and one from black.
Place the two ropes together, hold one end,
and twist the colors to make a two-tone rope
as shown in Photo C. Shape the rope around
the clay circle. Shape the ends into spirals for
the hanging loops. Roll two 1-inch clay ropes,
one from white and one from black. Place the
two ropes together, hold one end, and twist
the colors together to make a two-tone rope.
Coil the rope and place in the center of the
pendant. Bake the clay in the oven according
to the clay manufacturer's directions.
5 If desired paint the clay piece with a clear
acrylic sealer and let dry.
6 Thread the lacing through the loops at the
top of the pendant. Knot each lacing end
1½ inches from the end. Place a bead on each
lacing end and knot again. Knot the ends
together loosely to wear.

eyelet hearts pendant

A

B

C

beaded
ankle bracelets

Apply a
fresh coat of
nail polish
and show off
your dainty
foot jewelry!

leather lacing
ankle bracelet

fully beaded ankle bracelet

62

what you'll need

for leather lacing ankle bracelet
2 sterling silver crimp beads for leather
Crimping tool
1—12-inch piece of round purple leather lacing
1 medium sterling silver spring ring
2—3 mm sterling silver crimp beads
2—8 mm round sterling silver beads
1—8 mm lime green candy cane glass bead
1 medium sterling silver split ring

here's how

1 Flatten the leather crimp bead firmly on one end of the lacing. Attach the spring ring.
2 Thread 3 mm crimp bead, 8 mm round sterling silver bead, candy cane bead, 8 mm round sterling silver bead, and 3 mm crimp bead. Position candy cane bead in center of lacing. Flatten crimp beads on each side of silver beads.
3 Attach the leather crimp bead on other end; flatten firmly. Attach the split ring to the square part of the flattened crimp bead.

what you'll need

for fully beaded ankle bracelet
1—12-inch piece of .019 diameter beading wire
1 sterling silver spring ring clasp and jump ring
32—4 mm liquid sterling silver tubes
72 light purple seed beads
8 small peridot stone beads; 1 purple E bead
Wire cutters; 2—2 mm sterling silver crimp beads

here's how

1 Thread wire through a crimp bead, clasp, and back through bead; flatten crimp bead.
2 String beads in the following repeating order:
   1 silver tube
   3 seed beads
   1 silver tube
   3 seed beads
   1 silver tube
   3 seed beads
   1 silver tube
   1 peridot stone bead
Repeat for half the distance of the bracelet. String 1 peridot bead, 1 E bead, and 1 peridot bead. Repeat the first pattern.
3 Thread a crimp bead on end. Pass wire through jump ring and back through crimp

dangling ankle bracelet

bead in opposite direction; flatten. Trim the excess wire.

what you'll need

for dangling ankle bracelet
9—2.5 mm round sterling silver beads
2—Bali sterling silver shells
Wire cutters; needle-nose pliers
2—4 mm square orange glass beads
2—4 mm diamond-shape orange crystal beads
1—6 mm diamond-shape orange crystal bead
1—8 mm disk-shape orange crystal bead
5 sterling silver headpins
1—8-inch fine sterling silver chain
1—sterling silver spring ring clasp and jump ring

here's how

1 Place beads on two headpins as follows:
   1—2.5 mm round sterling silver bead
   1 Bali sterling silver shell
   1—2.5 mm round sterling silver bead
Clip headpin to ⅜ inch and bend at a 90-degree angle. Curve end into a loop using pliers. Leave an open space, attach to bracelet, and close.
2 For next headpin thread beads as follows:
   1—2.5 mm round sterling silver bead
   1—4 mm square orange glass bead
   1—4 mm orange crystal bead
   1—2.5 mm round silver bead
3 Fill two more headpins, adding the remaining beads as you wish.
4 Attach the beaded headpins to the bracelet, alternating orange and silver.
5 Attach a clasp to one end of chain and a jump ring to the other.

tickle
your toes

With all these rings to choose from, fashion a toe ring to coordinate with any outfit.

beads-all-around toe ring

by-the-sea toe ring

dangle-bead toe ring

artistic toe ring

totally-silver toe ring

what you'll need

for the beads-all-around toe ring

Piece of clear elastic cord
Approximately 30 black glass seed beads
1 rose crystal bead
Strong glue, such as E6000
Toothpick

here's how

1 Thread enough seed beads on elastic to fit around the top section of your toe.
2 Slide on the crystal bead.
3 Make a square knot by folding the elastic right over left and left over right.
4 Dab the end with a small touch of glue using a toothpick. Trim off the excess elastic and hide the knot in a bead.

what you'll need

for the by-the-sea toe ring

¾-inch sterling silver endless hoop earring
3 sterling silver crimp beads; crimping tool
2 large blue-green seed beads
2 large blue seed beads
1—4 mm sterling silver round bead

here's how

1 Open earring slightly. Add one crimp bead on the thin part of the hoop.
2 Thread on a blue-green seed bead, a blue seed bead, the silver bead, and a crimp bead; flatten the crimp bead.
3 Thread on a blue seed bead, a blue-green seed bead, and a crimp bead; flatten.

what you'll need

for the dangle-bead toe ring

¾-inch sterling silver endless hoop earring
2 sterling silver crimp beads; crimping tool
1 sterling silver 2-inch headpin
1—6 mm hemalyke (synthetic hematite) bead
Needle-nose pliers

here's how

1 Open earring slightly. Add one crimp bead on the thin part of the hoop.
2 Place hemalyke bead on the headpin. Using needle-nose pliers, make a right angle about ¼ inch above the bead. Cut off the headpin, leaving 1 inch. Use pliers to make a small loop about ⅛ inch above the bead and wrap the wire around the headpin; trim off excess.
3 Slip the hemalyke bead on the thin part of the loop. Add a crimp bead and flatten. Close the earring.

what you'll need

for the artistic toe ring

4—3 mm glass or semiprecious stone beads
6-inch piece of 20-gauge sterling silver wire
⅔-inch wood dowel; needle-nose pliers
Strong glue, such as E6000

here's how

1 Position one stone on the end of the wire. Using needle-nose pliers, pinch the tip of the wire and turn one full circle.
2 Using a ⅔-inch wood dowel or tube, bend the wire 2½ times around the dowel.
3 Slide on two beads, placing a bead on each wire.
4 Take the other end of the wire and repeat Step 1. Make two full twists for a more decorative end.
5 Using a toothpick, dab a small dot of glue directly on the decorative end. Slide a bead onto the glue.
6 Repeat the gluing process with the other two beads, staggering the distance between the beads. Let the glue dry.

what you'll need

for the totally-silver toe ring

1—¾-inch sterling silver endless hoop earring
2—3 mm round sterling silver bead
1—4 mm round sterling silver bead
2 sterling silver crimp beads; crimping tool

here's how

1 Open earring slightly.
2 Slide a crimp on the narrow wire and flatten. Thread on one 3 mm bead, the 4 mm bead, a 3 mm bead, and the crimp bead.
3 Close earring and flatten the crimp bead.

color wheel
scissors tails

Keep your
scissors handy
and protected with
a beaded tip cover
clipped to the
handle.

For a variation, use neutral-tone beads for the scissors protector chain.

what you'll need

2—2 mm sterling silver crimp beads
1—8- to 10-inch piece of .018-inch diameter stainless-steel beading wire
1 large gold-plated lobster clasp
Crimping tool; wire cutters
3—10 mm round rainbow miracle beads
1—10 mm round red miracle bead
1—10 mm round orange miracle bead
1—10 mm round yellow miracle bead
1—10 mm round green miracle bead
1—10 mm round blue miracle bead
1—10 mm round violet miracle bead
2 dark red crystal rondelle spacer beads
1 dark orange crystal rondelle spacer bead
1 dark green crystal rondelle spacer bead
1 dark blue crystal rondelle spacer bead
1 dark violet crystal rondelle spacer bead
1 light yellow crystal rondelle spacer bead
1 clear crystal rondelle spacer bead
5—4 mm golden glass beads
3—6 mm gold-plated saucer spacer beads
2—6 mm gold-plated tube spacer beads
1 small screw eye
1 medium knitting needle protector tip
1 stork-style scissors

here's how

1 Thread a crimp bead on one end of the beading wire and pass wire through the end of the lobster clasp. Run wire back through the crimp bead in the opposite direction. Flatten the crimp bead firmly. Trim the wire end.
2 Lay out the miracle beads, arranging them like the color wheel if desired. Alternate the miracle beads with the crystal rondelle beads.
3 Using golden beads on each end, thread the beads on the wire.
4 Thread a crimp bead on end of wire and pass it through screw eye. Run wire back through crimp bead in opposite direction. Flatten crimp bead. Trim the end.
5 Twist the screw eye into the end of the knitting needle protector tip. Clip the lobster clasp onto the scissors handle.

key chain candy

Always know where your keys are when they are attached to a glistening stream of candy-color beads.

what you'll need

12 mm jump ring
1- to 1½-inch diameter key ring
Jewelry pliers
16-inch piece of 26 lb. test beading string
Assortment of large and small glass and
    crystal beads and metal spacers
1 crimp bead
Crimping tool
Scissors

here's how

1 Place jump ring on key ring and close with jewelry pliers.

2 Fold string in half and loop over jump ring. Pull the loose ends through the loop tightly.

3 Thread both strands through the beads in the desired order. If you wish, thread identical small beads on each string end, then thread both strings through a large bead to make a pattern.

4 When beading is completed, add a crimp bead and crush. Cut off any excess beading string.

two-strand necklace

In minutes make a pretty choker that gently wraps your neck.

what you'll need

Turquoise glass rocaille E beads
Assorted lime green beads
2-tier cable necklace (available with beading
  supplies)
4 crimp beads
Crimping tool

here's how

❶ String beads onto wires, placing lime green beads between 8 to 10 turquoise beads. Leave ⅓ inch of wire at each end.
❷ Place wires through a crimp bead, through clasp, and run back into crimp bead. Squeeze crimp bead closed.

candy cane necklace

Candy canes come in all colors when you're talking beads, so make this sweet necklace using any combination you like.

what you'll need

- 2—crimp beads
- 1—24-inch piece of beading wire
- 1—6 mm spring ring clasp
- Crimping tool
- 13—glass candy cane beads
- 8—4 mm round silver beads
- 10—6 mm round silver beads
- 62—6 mm silver spacers
- 2—4 mm cat's-eye beads
- 6—6 mm cat's-eye beads
- Wire cutters
- 1—6 mm jump ring

here's how

1 Thread a crimp bead on one end of the wire, pass it through the end of the spring ring clasp, and run the wire back through the crimp bead in the opposite direction. Flatten the crimp bead firmly. Trim the end.

2 Separating the candy cane beads with a silver or cat's-eye bead and four spacers, thread on beads in the desired pattern.

3 Thread a crimp bead on the end and pass the wire through the jump ring. Run the wire back through the crimp bead in the opposite direction. Flatten the crimp bead firmly. Trim the excess wire.

weekend
shopping pouch

Make a playful felt purse with beaded fringe to use when whimsy is the word of the day.

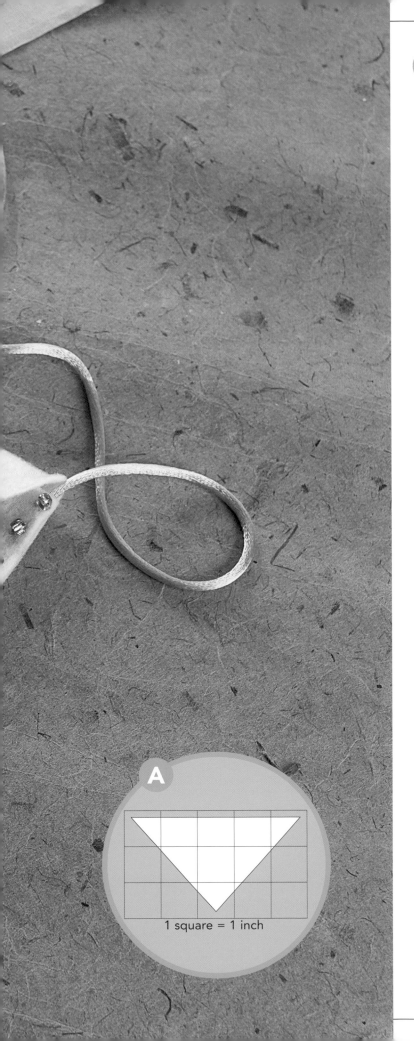

what you'll need

4½×13½-inch piece of lime green felt
Sharp scissors
Pins
Aqua thread
Needle
Aqua glass rocaille E beads
¼-inch-long lime green beads
1 yard of turquoise ratail cord
Turquoise embroidery floss, such as DMC 907
¾-inch-wide doughnut-shape aqua bead
Iron

here's how

❶ Using the pattern, *below left,* cut a point on one end of the felt piece. Fold the felt strip so that the point becomes a flap over the flat end. Pin sides.

❷ Thread needle with aqua thread and tie a knot in one end. Coming from between the layers, go through the felt at one end of the fold ¼ inch from the end. String one aqua bead, one lime bead, one aqua bead, one lime bead, and two aqua beads. Stitch back through the bead, starting at the second bead from the bottom. Push needle back through felt and come back out ¼ inch from the first beaded string. Bead another fringe, adding an additional aqua bead between the lime beads. Continue going across and adding one aqua bead with each string until you reach the center, which should have a total of eight aqua beads between the lime green beads. Continue the fringes going across the second half, decreasing the aqua beads by one on each fringe.

❸ Slide 1 inch of one end of the ratail cord between the felt layers at the top side. From inside push needle through cord and felt, thread on an aqua bead, thread back through felt and attach another bead to back side. Continue sewing beads every ⅓ inch down the side, sewing beads on the front and back. Repeat on the other side.

❹ Fold the flap over the purse front and iron the edge. Using six strands of embroidery floss, attach the doughnut-shape aqua bead to the center of the flap. Leave the floss loose in a ½-inch loop so that the bead dangles.

A

1 square = 1 inch

treasured
gems

This sophisticated piece of jewelry dresses up any outfit.

what you'll need

2-tier cable necklace; two 1-inch and one 1½-inch bead bars, such as Better Beads
Crystal glass rocaille E beads
Aqua glass rocaille E beads; yellow opaque E beads; red glass rocaille E beads
3—½-inch teardrop red beads; 2 beads each: disk turquoise, disk yellow, square red, oval lime, cylinder-shape aqua glass, and round red; crimp bead; crimping tool; jewelry pliers

here's how

1 With pliers cut the shorter strand from the necklace, leaving one strand.

2 Unscrew the top ball from longest bead bar. Slide on a teardrop red bead, two crystal E beads, two aqua beads, one yellow opaque bead, and two aqua beads. Screw ball on. On the two shorter bead bars, slide on one teardrop red bead, one crystal E bead, one aqua E bead, one yellow opaque bead, and one aqua bead. Screw balls on.

3 String on five crystal E beads, two red E beads, three crystal E beads, one turquoise disk, six crystal E beads, one disk yellow, six crystal E beads, one square red bead, six crystal E beads, one oval lime bead, six crystal E beads, one cylinder-shape aqua, six crystal E beads, one round red bead, six crystal E beads, one shorter bead bar, one crystal E bead, three red E beads, two crystal E beads, the longest bead bar, two crystal E beads, three red E beads, one crystal E bead and a short bead bar. Repeat stringing; reverse pattern starting with first bar.

4 Put wire end in crimp and squeeze closed.

daisy chain
necklace

Make rings of tiny seed beads with contrasting centers to resemble a chain of small flowers.

what you'll need

40-inch piece of beading thread
Beading needle; spring ring clasp
Size 11/0 seed beads in desired colors

here's how

1 Thread the needle onto the piece of thread.

2 Attach (knot) the spring ring clasp to the end of the beading thread. Make sure it is well-secured.

3 To make the first daisy, put on four "petal" beads. Next put on one "center" bead as shown in Diagram A, *below left*. Put the needle back through the first bead and pull tight as shown in Diagram B.

4 Put on two more "petal" beads as shown in Diagram C. Put the needle back through the petal bead next to the center bead as shown in Diagram D. Pull thread tight to make a daisy as shown in Diagram E.

5 Repeat Steps 3–4 using a different color of petal beads and center beads if desired.

6 Repeat Steps 3–6 over and over until the daisies are long enough to make a necklace.

7 Attach the jump ring on the end.

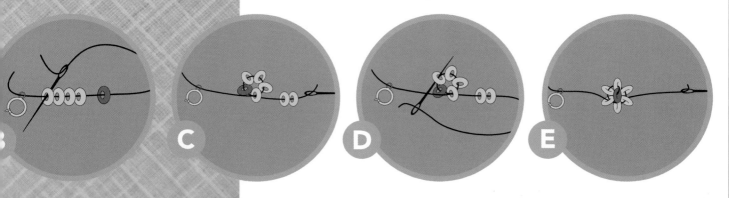

button-up
bracelets

Use a lovely antique button as a clasp for a vintage-looking bracelet.

Variety of beads and gold-tone spacers
12 inches of .015 clear C-Flex 49 strand
    beading wire or other thin, strong pliable
    beading wire
2 silver-plated or sterling silver crimp beads
20–25—3 mm seed beads to coordinate with
    other beads
Antique silver button with a shank or loop
    on back
Crimping tool or needle-nose pliers; scissors

here's how

1 Lay out beads and spacers in desired pattern, using silver spacers to highlight desired beads.

2 String 1 crimp bead, then approximately 14 seed beads on the wire. Working with threading end of wire, bring the end back through the crimp bead with 1 inch of wire hanging from end.

3 Push crimp bead up tightly against seed beads to form a loop. Hold tight with fingers and try to push the antique button through the loop. It should be a snug fit. If too big or too small, adjust loop by pulling wire back through crimp bead and adding or subtracting a few seed beads. Thread wire back through crimp bead and again pull tightly.

4 When fit is snug and button passes through loop, use crimping pliers or needle-nose pliers to squeeze the crimp bead closed.

5 String two or three seed beads onto the opposite end of wire, being sure to pass over extra wire protruding from the crimp bead. Then string the rest of the beads and spacers onto the wire.

6 Check length of bracelet by wrapping around wrist, being careful not to drop beads from loose end of wire. Beads should meet with the end of the seed bead loop. Add or subtract beads as necessary.

7 Add three seed beads to the wire, then the remaining crimp bead. Thread wire through the shank of the button, then back through the crimp bead and 1 inch of seed beads and regular beads.

8 Pull wire tight against the shank of the button. Squeeze crimp bead closed with pliers.

9 Carefully cut off remainder of wire with small scissors.

decorating
with beads

Make your surroundings
            glisten with creativity by applying
beaded accents to pillows,
            bookmarks, valances, glassware,
            candleholders, and more!

bookworm baubles

Hold your place in your next book with a fun and funky beaded wire bookmark that works up quicker than you can say "Once upon a time."

what you'll need

Wire cutters
18-gauge wire in desired color
Needle-nose pliers
Glass beads
Small dowel
36-gauge metallic wire, optional

here's how

1 Cut a 24-inch length of 18-gauge wire. Using pliers bend over one end of wire for the bottom of the bookmark.

2 Thread desired bead(s) on straight end of wire and slide them to the bottom. Shape the wire as desired.

3 For the top of the bookmark, make a bend in the wire or wrap it around a small dowel where you want the top beads to be held. Place beads on the wire. Shape the end of the wire into a spiral to hold the beads in place. If desired, make a wire spiral from a short length of wire and attach to the top of the bookmark by forming a loop in the end of the bookmark wire.

4 If desired tightly wrap small sections of the beaded bookmark with metallic wire.

a shade better

Lend pizzazz to ordinary lampshades using whatever colors coordinate with your style at home.

what you'll need

Black silk string; needle; scissors
Small blue pleated lampshade
80—4 mm light purple glass beads
44—6 mm disk-shape clear crystal beads
10—12 mm bumpy purple glass beads
20—4 mm square clear crystal beads

here's how

1 Knot silk string and begin sewing. Hide the knot between the blue shade and the white frame. Slide on beads at every inch and tack the beaded string to the outside of the shade until the shade is encircled.

2 For each beaded tassel knot the silk string and place one 6 mm disk, one bumpy purple bead, and one 4 mm square bead. Attach the tassel to the shade by stitching between the shade and frame. Continue moving the needle between the layers, spacing stitches approximately 1½ inches apart. Knot the thread and cut off any excess. Repeat the process until all tassels are evenly attached around the base of the lampshade.

what you'll need

for the golden lampshade

Light silk beading thread; needle; scissors
Smooth small light golden lampshade
Golden beads in a variety of shapes and sizes
Strong glue, such as E6000

here's how

1 Knot the thread and pull the needle from inside the frame to the outside top of the shade near the metal frame.

2 String approximately 2½ to 3 inches of beads, alternating a small or medium bead with a bugle bead. To loop beaded string firmly attach string to the top of the next section of metal frame, looping the string under the wire on the inside of the shade. If preferred glue the string to the top of the shade. Repeat this process for each piece of metal frame.

3 Select small and medium beads to glue around the top of the shade frame. Let the glue dry before moving the frame.

tassel time

Lovely and elegant, beaded tassels beautify doorknobs, drawer pulls, keys in locks, and anything else from which they dangle.

what you'll need

Spool of .010 diameter micro stainless-steel nylon-coated wire
Glass seed beads
8 medium-size ceramic beads
6 flat glass beads
12-inch length of 28-gauge wire
1—flat disk-shape bead
1—large ceramic bead
2—¼-inch diameter round ceramic beads

here's how

❶ Cut twelve 11-inch lengths of nylon-coated wire. To begin each strand slip one seed bead on the end of the wire and knot wire around the bead to secure the end.

❷ String 8 inches of seed beads on each wire. Knot the wire around the last seed bead and cut off the excess wire.

❸ Cut four 11-inch strands of wire. Begin with a seed bead, thread on a medium ceramic bead, and continue with seed beads; end with another ceramic bead and seed bead. Knot off the end. These strands should measure 9 inches.

❹ Cut three 10-inch lengths of wire. Begin and end these strands with a flat glass bead and seed bead. Make these strands 6 inches.

❺ Stack the 19 strands of beads together. Fold the piece of 28-gauge wire in half and slip around the center of all the strands of beads. Twist the wire together and push through the disk-shape bead, large ceramic bead, and one of the ¼-inch round beads.

❻ For the loop string seed beads on each of the wire ends, stopping 1 inch from the ends. Bring the two wire ends together and slip them through the remaining ¼-inch bead. Slip one of the wire ends around and back up through the bead. Finish off by twisting the wire ends together and flatten them against the top of the bead. Cut off the excess wire.

charmed, I'm sure

Wrapping your stemware with jewelry looks elegant and helps your companions remember which glass is theirs.

what you'll need

¾-inch-circumference wire hoops
Round-nose pliers
Assorted glass beads
1½-inch golden headpins
Wire cutters
Large wire hoop

here's how

① To make a dozen wineglass charms, choose 12 wire hoops. Bend the straight end of each wire hoop into a hook using the round-nose pliers.

② Select beads for each charm and begin threading beads on headpins. Trim wire down with wire cutters to ⅜ inch. Bend the end of the headpin into a loop using the round-nose pliers. Slip each beaded headpin onto a small wire hoop.

③ When finished thread all beaded charms onto one large wire hoop and bend the straight end of the large wire hoop into a hook using the round-nose pliers.

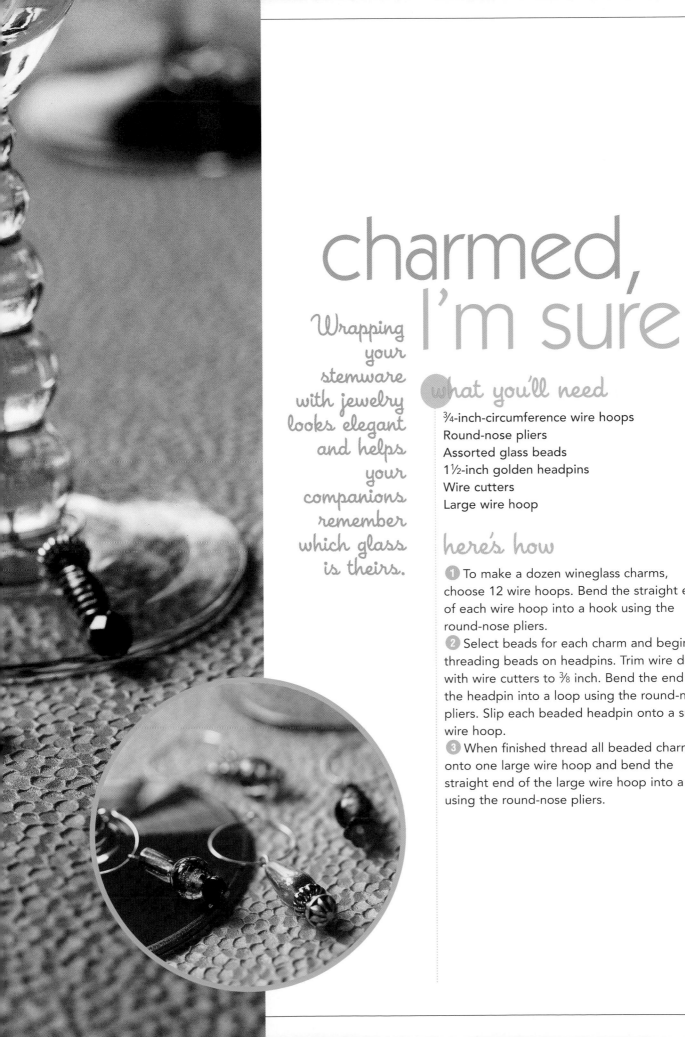

sunshine
pillow

Bring a ray
of warmth to
any room of
the house with
this cheerful
toss pillow.

what you'll need

60 inches of cream silk beading cord; needle
48—dark red bicone glass beads
20—6 mm orange miracle beads
48—dark golden bicone glass beads
30–40 seed beads; 3—4 mm golden bugle beads
24—6 mm golden miracle beads
12-inch square pillow; yellow sewing thread
3—3 mm crimp beads; glue, such as E6000
9–12 decorative beads in orange and red

here's how

1 Using silk beading cord bead as follows:
   1—red bicone bead
   1—orange miracle bead
   1—golden bicone bead
   2—seed beads
   1—red bicone bead
   1—golden miracle bead
   1—golden bicone bead
   3—seed beads
Repeat pattern until 44 inches long.
2 Sew beads to the top lip of the pillow, starting with a red bicone bead in the corner. Using yellow sewing thread attach the string to all pillow sides, tacking every inch.
3 For tassel, cut a 4-inch piece of cord. Crimp a bead on the end. Bead as follows:
   1—golden bugle bead
   1—orange miracle bead
   1—large orange decorative bead
   1—clear red bead
   1—large golden bicone bead
   1—large red bicone bead
4 Cut a 6-inch piece of thread. Crimp the bottom. Bead as follows:
   1—golden bugle bead
   1—large orange bead
   1—oblong clear red bead
   1—orange miracle bead
   1—large golden bicone
   1—orange miracle bead
   1—red bicone bead
5 Repeat with a 4-inch piece of thread. Bead as follows:
   1 medium clear red glass bead
   1 large orange decorative bead
   1 large clear red bead
   1 large golden bicone bead
6 Knot each tassel to a corner of the pillow. Use a dab of glue to attach other beads to the top of the tassel as desired.

91

fine-line bookmarks

Create a special bookmark by beading a narrow string of silver and saving large colorful beads for the ends.

what you'll need

19 inches of .019-inch-diameter beading wire
2 crimp beads
Desired color beads for ends
Crimping tool
Approximately 20—3 mm round beads
Approximately 20—15 mm tube beads
Desired small beads for center

here's how

❶ Thread a crimp bead on one end of wire. Pass the wire through the end of the desired bottom bead and back through the crimp bead in the opposite direction. Flatten the crimp bead firmly. Trim the end.

❷ Thread on beads in the desired order, using color beads at the bookmark ends and the 3 mm round and 15 mm tube beads (along with other desired small beads) for the center of the bookmark.

❸ When the beading is complete, flatten a crimp bead on the end. Trim the excess wire.

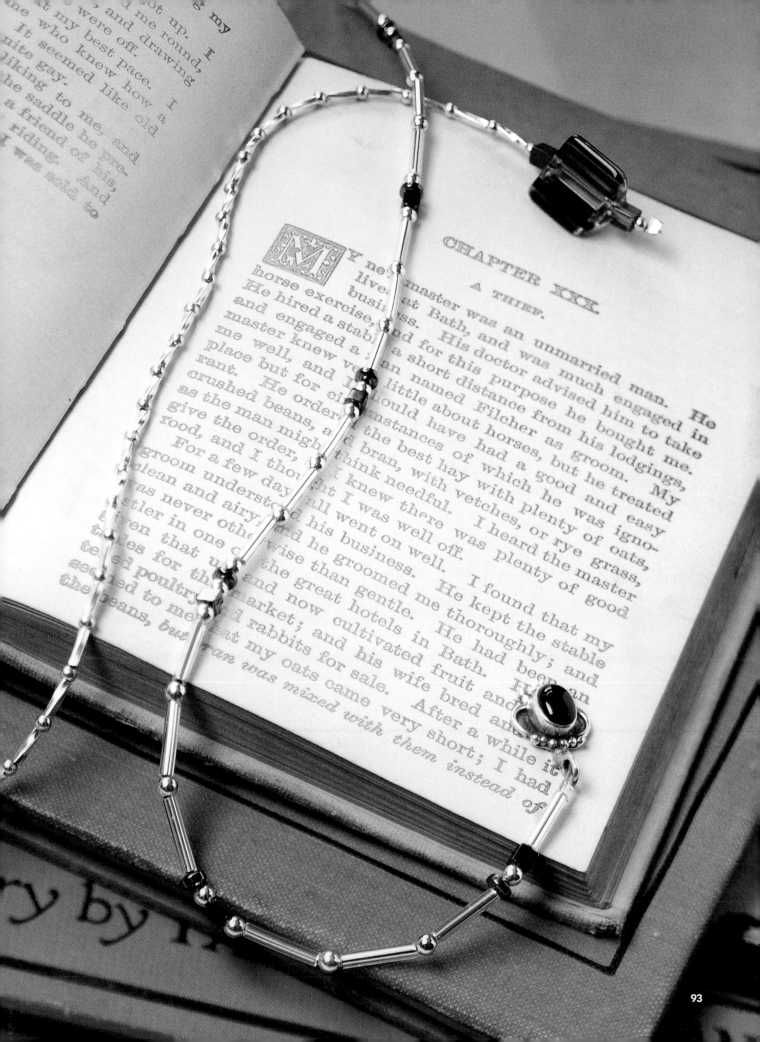

enlightened
pull chains

Make functional pull chains pretty by camouflaging the chains with an assortment of glass beads.

light pull chains

three-strand ceiling fan chain

what you'll need

for light pull chains

28-gauge wire; wire cutters
Assorted sizes and colors of beads
Needle-nose pliers; crimp beads; ball chain

here's how

1 Cut a 16-inch length of wire.

2 Arrange assorted sizes and colors of beads for a pleasing pattern. String beads on the wire. Wrap one end several times to keep beads from slipping off.

3 Put a crimp on the wire next to the bottom bead. Using pliers, squeeze the crimp flat to secure the beads. Fold excess wire and run back through several beads; then cut the excess off.

4 At other end, put a crimp next to the top bead and squeeze with pliers to secure beads. Cut wire, leaving ½ inch. Take the cover off a ball chain and wrap the wire end around the end of the chain. Replace cover. Take the chain joining piece off one end and cut ball chain to desired length. Replace the joining piece.

5 For the variation, *right*, bead three 6-inch pieces of wire and repeat Step 4, placing a crimp bead over all three wires.

what you'll need

for the three-strand ceiling fan chain

28-gauge wire; wire cutters
Assorted sizes and colors of beads
2—1-inch-long aqua glass beads
3 oval orange beads
Opaque E beads in yellow and orange
3 round yellow beads
Crimp beads; crimping tool
Ball chain

here's how

1 Cut three pieces of wire 16 inches long. Twist the three strands together on one end to hold and prevent beads from sliding off. String six beads of various sizes and colors on all three strands of wire. Separate the wires and string 12 yellow opaque E beads on each of the three wires. String 5 various beads on the three wires together, then separate the wires and string 12 orange opaque E beads on each wire. String 3 assorted beads on the three wires together. Separate wires and string eight yellow opaque beads, and then one oval orange bead on each wire.

2 Put a crimp on each wire and push next to the orange bead. Squeeze the crimp flat to secure the beads. Fold excess wire and run back through several beads. Cut off the excess.

3 At other end, put a crimp next to the top bead and squeeze with pliers to secure beads. Cut wire, leaving ½ inch. Take the cover off a ball chain and wrap the wire end around the end of the chain. Replace cover. Take the chain-joining piece off one end and cut ball chain to the desired length. Replace the joining piece.

light pull chain variation

95

glorious gourd

Wire a beaded fringe on the rim of one of Mother Nature's lovely creations.

what you'll need

90 inches of colored wire; wire cutters
30–40—3 mm golden seed beads
1 gourd bowl, approximately 9 inches in diameter, with predrilled holes around wrapped woven rim
2–3 packages of assorted glass beads
8–10 white bone beads
Crimp beads and crimping tool, optional

here's how

1 Cut a 6-inch piece of wire. Secure a seed bead on one end of the wire by twisting the wire around it. From inside the bowl, thread the wire through a predrilled hole, allowing the seed bead to secure the wire.

2 String on beads, using a variety of sizes, textures, and colors.

3 When 1½ inches of string is beaded, thread the white bone bead. Crimp the wire with a crimp bead or wrap the wire end tightly around a seed bead. Trim off the excess wire.

4 Repeat around the bowl. Alternate beads as desired. Place a white bone bead to every other string.

pleated sachet pillows

what you'll need

for the golden sachet
Ruler
Pins
¼ yard golden silk fabric; scissors
Golden thread
Sewing machine
Sewing needle
Golden glass rocaille E beads
12—¼-inch cylinder-shape green glass beads
4—10 mm round green beads
Fiberfill
Potpourri, optional
Iron

here's how

1 From golden fabric, cut a 4½-inch square for the back and 4½×10-inch rectangle for the front. Fold the rectangle into ½-inch pleats horizontally and press. Trim front to match the back if necessary. Pin the right sides together and stitch using a ¼-inch seam allowance and leaving a 2-inch opening along one unpleated edge.

2 Turn right side out and press. Stitch golden glass beads at ½-inch intervals around edge of sachet.

3 At corners, secure thread and make three strands for beads. Bead each center strand as follows:
    5 golden beads
    1 cylinder-shape green bead
    4 golden beads
    1 round green bead
    1 golden bead
Insert thread back through beads starting with the round green bead. For each side strand, bead as follows:
    12 golden beads
    1 green cylinder bead
    1 golden bead
Insert thread back through beads from bottom, starting with the green bead.

4 Stuff pillow lightly with fiberfill and potpourri if desired. Whipstitch the opening closed.

what you'll need

for the silver sachet
¼ yard silver silk fabric
Scissors; pins
Gray thread
Sewing machine
Needle
Crystal glass rocaille E beads
16—¼-inch oval purple beads
4 aqua cylinder beads
Fiberfill
Iron

here's how

1 From silver fabric, cut a 4½-inch square for the back and 8½-inch square for the front. Fold fabric diagonally to form a 1½-inch-wide tuck with one ½-inch-wide tuck on each side. Trim front to match the back if necessary. Pin the right sides together and stitch using a ¼-inch seam allowance and leaving a 2-inch opening along one unpleated edge.

2 Turn right side out and press. Sew crystal glass beads at ½-inch intervals around the edge of the sachet.

3 At corners, secure thread and make three strands for beads. Bead each center strand as follows:
    4 crystal beads
    1 purple bead
    2 crystal beads
    1 purple bead
    2 crystal beads
    1 aqua bead
    2 crystal beads
Insert thread back through beads, starting with the second crystal bead from the bottom. For each side strand, bead as follows:
12 crystal beads
    1 purple bead
    1 crystal bead
Insert thread back through beads, starting with the purple bead. Secure thread.

4 Stuff lightly with fiberfill and whipstitch opening closed.

overjoyed ornaments

Beaded centers give these clear glass teardrop ornaments a festive, contemporary look.

what you'll need

20-gauge golden wire
Wire cutters
Round-nose pliers
Colorful glass beads
Clear glass teardrop ornaments

here's how

1 Cut one 20-inch-long piece of wire. Coil one end of wire using round-nose pliers and begin threading glass beads.

2 Snip a 7-inch-long piece of wire and thread it in amongst some of the beads. Coil each end of the 7-inch wire and continue threading beads on the long wire.

3 Remove the top of the ornament. Lower the strand of beads into the glass ornament. Attach the ornament cap and thread the remaining wire up through ornament cap. Thread on one additional bead and coil the remaining wire.

dazzling
bottle

Pick out a glass vase in a favorite hue and wrap the neck with wire and interesting beaded fringe.

what you'll need

2-inch golden split ring
Purple bottle
9 decorative coins in various sizes
1 thick golden coin with large hole
24 inches of golden elastic cord
Scissors
2 large oblong antique cream beads
3—8 mm cylinder-shape golden beads
2 oblong bone beads
6 ornate dark blue beads with golden marks
7 vintage dark golden beads in any shape
Strong glue, such as E6000
8 round purple glass beads in various sizes
1—3-inch headpin
Needle-nose pliers
Wire cutters
1—2-inch headpin
1 ornate 10 mm square bead with rhinestones

here's how

1 Carefully pull apart the split ring, making an S shape. Wrap the wire around the neck of the bottle.

2 Thread a regular and a thick coin on the wire.

3 Cut two 12-inch pieces of golden elastic cord. Fold each cord in half. Attach each cord to the wire by pulling the cord ends through the loop.

4 Bead the first piece of cord in the following order:
- 1—large antique cream bead
- 1—8 mm golden bead
- 1—oblong bone bead
- 1—coin
- 1—dark blue bead
- 1—vintage dark golden bead
- 1—oblong bone bead
- 1—coin
- 1—dark blue bead

5 Tie a knot in the end of the cord and trim off the excess. Apply a dot of glue to the end of the cord.

6 For the second cord, thread beads in the following order:
- 1—8 mm golden bead
- 1—purple bead
- 1—coin
- 1—dark blue bead
- 1—purple bead
- 1—8 mm golden bead

- 1—large dark blue bead
- 1—coin
- 1 purple bead

Tie a knot in cord, trim, and dot with glue.

7 For the third cord, bead as follows:
- 1 large purple bead
- 1 coin
- 1 dark blue bead
- 1 vintage dark golden bead
- 1 coin
- 1 dark blue bead
- 1 vintage dark golden bead
- 1 purple bead
- 1 coin
- 1 vintage dark golden bead
- 1 purple bead

Tie a knot in cord, trim, and dot with glue.

8 For the fourth cord, thread beads in the following order:
- 1 vintage dark golden bead
- 1 large purple bead
- 1 coin
- 1 vintage dark golden bead

Tie a knot in cord, trim, and dot with glue.

9 Place a vintage dark golden bead, large cream bead, and purple bead on the 3-inch headpin. With needle-nose pliers, bend the headpin wire to a right angle and clip off the wire to leave a ⅜-inch end. Use pliers to form a loop at the end of the headpin. String the loop on the split ring.

10 Place a 10 mm square bead on the 2-inch headpin. Bend the wire to a right angle and clip off the wire to leave a ⅜-inch end. Use pliers to form a loop at the end of the headpin. String the loop on the split ring.

dress-up shade

Give a splash of color to any room with a felt-covered lampshade trimmed with glistening beads.

what you'll need

Pencil; 4-inch adhesive lampshade
Aqua and pink threads; needle
Aqua glass rocaille E beads
Pink glass rocaille E beads
6 mm round turquoise beads
Light yellow felt; sharp scissors

here's how

1 Make a pencil mark every 2 inches on the bottom edge of the shade. Using aqua thread, insert the needle through the back of the shade slightly above one of the pencil marks. String on 25 aqua beads and insert needle through the shade slightly above the next mark. Pull the thread so beads snug up to the bottom edge of the shade. Wrap thread under edge of shade and insert needle back through the same hole in the shade to secure. Continue threading aqua beads in this manner around shade.

2 With pencil, mark center points between the two ends of the turquoise loops.

3 Thread needle with pink thread. Insert needle through shade from back slightly above one of the pencil marks. String on 11 pink beads, a large turquoise bead, and 11 more pink beads. Insert needle back through the shade slightly above the next pencil mark and secure as for the aqua beads. Repeat around shade.

4 Using the pattern that came with lampshade, cut a shade cover from the yellow felt. Sew aqua beads onto the shade at regular intervals from the center of the shade down.

5 Remove protective paper from the shade. Press the felt into the adhesive around shade.

6 With the pencil, make marks at 2-inch intervals around the top edge.

7 With aqua thread, poke up from the back of shade near the top at one of the marks. String on 25 aqua beads and sew back through at the next mark. Secure thread and repeat to make the loops around the top of the shade.

8 With pink thread, insert needle from the back between the aqua loops. String on 10 pink beads, 1 turquoise bead, and 10 more pink beads. Insert needle back through the shade next to where the strand started. Secure thread and cut. Repeat between the remaining aqua loops.

bath salts
bottle

Give a gift of relaxation—bath salts presented in a oceanic bead-trimmed bottle.

what you'll need

24 inches of beading wire
Variety of beads, including seed, miracle, silver, clear crystal, bugle, and citron chips
2 crimp beads
Crimping tool
Square green bottle
3 headpins
Needle-nose pliers
2 golden shell beads
3 cups scented green bath salts
Cork stopper

here's how

1 Bead 18 inches of wire with a variety of beads.
2 Crimp both ends with a crimp bead. Wrap the wire around the neck of the bottle.
3 Create dangles by threading the headpins with an assortment of beads. Place a shell on two of the headpins. Leave approximately ½ inch at the end. Loop the end around the wire to attach the dangle to the bottle.
4 Arrange the dangles as desired. Fill bottle with salts and insert stopper.

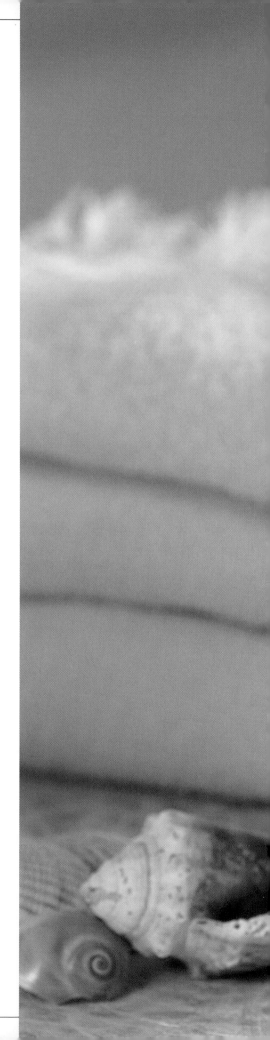

sunshine valance

Beaded details, including loops, dots, fringe, and a tassel, enhance the hems of this two-layer valance.

what you'll need

Fabric in 2 prints; tape measure; scissors
Sewing machine
Sewing thread; contrasting large rickrack
Needle; large seed beads to coordinate with fabric; small metallic golden beads
½-inch-long metallic golden tube beads
Metallic golden beaded fringe trim

here's how

1 Determine the desired valance width and length, including ½-inch seam allowances. For the length, double the desired measurement and subtract 6 inches. Cut both fabrics this size. Cut one end of both fabric pieces into a V. With right sides together, sew along the edges, leaving an opening for turning; turn. Sew opening closed. Sew rickrack along the V.

2 Hand-sew a bead to each rickrack point, alternating seed and golden round beads.

3 To make loops, thread seven metallic golden beads on thread and stitch to edge of rickrack. Make five loops on each side of point.

4 For each tassel length, insert needle from back of flap point. Thread on three seed beads, one tube bead, three seed beads, one golden bead, and a seed bead. Insert the needle back through beads, starting with the golden bead.

5 Make a long beaded loop to hang below tassel using seed, tube, and round beads.

6 For hem trim, sew on alternating tube and seed beads. Sew fringe to bottom of valance. Fold flap over and sew the rod pocket seam.

sources

project designers

Susan M. Banker—pages 42–46,
    52–53, 56–61, 82–83, and 108–109.
Elizabeth Dahlstrom—pages 76–77.
Kristen Dietrich—pages 88–89 and
    100–101.
Phyllis Dobbs—pages 70, 72–75,
    94–95, 98–99, and 104–105.
Phyllis Dunstan—pages 86–87.
Veronica Guzman & Betsy May—
    pages 78–79.
Jan Kuhl—pages 24–39, 48–49,
    62–69, 71, 84–85, 90–93, 95–97,
    102–103, and 106–107.
Pam Kvitne—pages 40–41 and 50–51.
Julie Streets—page 39.
Alice Wetzel—pages 22–23, 47, and 54–55.

special thanks to:

Tami Rupiper, pages 14–15.
Alice and Butch Wetzel, pages16–19.

beads

A Touch of Glass, Cousin Corp.
P.O. Box 2939
Largo, FL 33779
Orders—Customer Service:
800/366-2687
800/366-6121 (FAX)
custserv@cousin.com

Hirschburg Schutz & Co.
650 Liberty Avenue
Union, NJ 07083
908/810-1111

Mill Hill, Inc.
Division of Gay Bowles Sales
P.O. Box 1060
Janesville, WI 53547
608/754-6665 (FAX)

cable

Elite Better Beads
Hirschburg Schutz & Co.
650 Liberty Avenue
Union, NJ 07083
908/810-1111

embroidery floss

Anchor Consumer Service Dept.
P.O. Box 27067
Greenville, SC 29616

DMC
Port Kearney Building 10
South Kearney, NJ 07032-0650

headpins

Elite Better Beads
Hirschberg Schutz & Co. Inc.
Union, NJ 07083

lampshades

Kiti Lampshade
Woodstock Wire Works, Inc.
300 N. Seminary Avenue
Woodstock, IL 60098
815/338-8158

lots-o-stuff

Bead Creative
906½ 42nd Street
Des Moines, Iowa 50312
515/255-3363

colors

birthstones

January	Garnet
February	Amethyst
March	Aquamarine
April	Diamond
May	Emerald
June	Pearl
July	Ruby
August	Peridot
September	Sapphire
October	Opal
November	Topaz
December	Turquoise

symbolic colors

Pink	Breast Cancer
Teal	Ovarian Cancer
Clear	Lung Cancer
Blue	Prostate Cancer
Black	Melanoma
Purple	Pancreatic Cancer
Orange	Leukemia
Gray	Brain Cancer
Brown	Colon Cancer
Burgundy	Multiple Myeloma
Golden	Childhood Cancer
Lavender	General Cancer Awareness

references

bibliography

the Bead History section, pages 6-7

*African Crafts by Jane Kerina (Sayre Publishing, 1970).

*American Indian Beadwork by W. Ben Hunt and J.F. "Buck" Burshears (Collier Books, 1951).

*Ethnic Dress: A Comprehensive Guide to the Folk Costume of the World by Frances Kennett (Facts On File, 1994).

*Fashion Bead Embroidery by Natalie Giltsoff (Batsford/Branford, 1971).

*Maggie Lane's Book of Beads by Maggie Lane (Charles Scribner's Sons, 1979).

*Victoriana Americana by Evelyn Swenson (Greatlakes Living Press, 1976).

index

beading projects